say goodbye to WHINING, COMPLAINING, and bad Attitudes... in you and your kids

Scott Turansky, D.Min., and
Joanne Miller, R.N., B.S.N.

WATERBROOK
PRESS

Say Goodbye to Whining, Complaining,
and Bad Attitudes...in You and Your Kids

PUBLISHED BY WATERBROOK PRESS
12265 Oracle Boulevard, Suite 200
Colorado Springs, Colorado 80921

All scripture quotations, unless otherwise indicated, are taken from the
Holy Bible, New International Version®. NIV®. Copyright © 1973, 1978, 1984
by International Bible Society. Used by permission of Zondervan Publishing
House. All rights reserved.

The names of persons who have come to *Effective Parenting* for counseling have
been changed. Some illustrations are a combination of individual stories to
protect confidentiality.

Stories of the authors' children have been used by permission.

ISBN 978-0-87788-354-8

Copyright © 2000 by Scott Turansky and Joanne Miller

All rights reserved. No part of this book may be reproduced or transmitted
in any form or by any means, electronic or mechanical, including photocopying
and recording, or by any information storage and retrieval system, without
permission in writing from the publisher.

Published in the United States by WaterBrook Multnomah, an imprint of the Crown Publishing Group,
a division of Random House Inc., New York.

WATERBROOK and its deer colophon are registered trademarks of Random House Inc.

The Turanskys and the Millers founded the ministry of *Effective Parenting*,
a nonprofit corporation committed to the communication of sound biblical
parenting principles through teaching, counseling, and the publication of written,
audio, and video materials. More information about *Effective Parenting* may be found
at http://www.effectiveparenting.org.

Library of Congress Cataloging-in-Publication Data
Turansky, Scott, 1957-
    Say goodbye to whining, complaining, and bad attitudes :...in you and your kids'/
Scott Turansky and Joanne Miller.
        p. cm.
    "A Shaw book published by WaterBrook Press"—CIP t.p. verso.
    ISBN 0-87788-354-8
    1. Parenting—United States.   2. Parents—United States—Attitudes.   3. Children—
United States—Attitudes.   4. Honor.   I. Miller, Joanne, 1960-

HQ755.83 .T87 2000
649'.1—dc21

                                                            00-055662

Printed in the United States of America

2011

20 19 18 17

Praise for *Say Goodbye to Whining*

"This is the best book on the subject I have ever read. I need it, my kids need it, and you need it! It will do *wonders* for your attitude and your children. Barbara and I could have really used this fifteen years ago, but you can use it today."

—DENNIS RAINEY, executive director of FamilyLife

"These two gifted authors have gone beyond the simplistic suggestions found in so many parenting books and have uncovered the real secret of producing lasting change in our children. I enthusiastically recommend this book to any parent who wants to experience genuine transformation in their home."

—DR. ROBERT JEFFRESS, pastor and author of
When Forgiveness Doesn't Make Sense

"Our listeners at New Life love this book. The principles work—I know, because I've used them in my own family and have seen great results!"

—STEPHEN ARTERBURN, author of *Toxic Faith* and
founder of Women of Faith conferences

"If you yearn for your family to communicate with love and honor, if your prayer is for children who desire to serve others rather than serving themselves, if you want to laugh often and feel more real joy in raising your children, read this book. It changed my family from the very first day we put its principles to work."

—SANDRA BYRD, best-selling children's book author and
frequent contributor to *Christian Parenting Today*

"As I've implemented the ideas in *Say Goodbye to Whining*, I've seen dramatic changes in our children and myself. The book has lived up to its name! Most important, we have a family attempting to truly honor each other and the Lord in everyday life."
— ANN KROEKER, author of *The Contemplative Mom*

"Our family is using *Say Goodbye to Whining* during our family devotions. Our kids are getting the hang of what it means to honor each other—and Mom and Dad are catching on too! This is a book that can change the emotional climate of your home."
— BOB LEPINE, co-host of FamilyLife Today

"No more slapping a Band-Aid on poor family dynamics. This book will enable you to get to the root of your family's communication struggles and create a loving, supportive environment. Turansky and Miller dig beneath the surface of family life and show us how to get what we really want: peace, honor, and cooperation in our homes from the inside out."
— GEOFF AND JANET BENGE, authors of numerous books, including several titles in the Christian Heroes series of biographies

"If you are tired of all the legalistic child-training books and programs that focus on parents maintaining control with superficial solutions, you will want to apply this book's life-changing principles in your relationships. The emphasis on honor in *Say Goodbye to Whining* addresses the heart-related issues that bring lasting change."
— MARILYN HOWSHALL, author of *Wisdom's Way of Learning* and developer of the Lifestyle of Learning approach to home education

To Carrie from Scott...

I thank you for your patience, encouragement, and support
as I've worked many hours on this book.
I'm also grateful for the many things I've learned about honor from you.
And to my children, Josh, Melissa, Ben, Elizabeth, and Megan,
for helping me learn how to implement honor in the family.

———————

To Ed from Joanne...

I am grateful for your steadfast belief in me and in this project.
Your encouragement and enthusiasm for this book
have inspired me day after day.
Your life example of honor has transformed our family.
And to my children, David and Tim,
thank you for your participation in this pilgrimage toward honor.

contents

Acknowledgments

We thank Fred Miller for his friendship and teaching on the family. The ideas for chapter 10 have been inspired by him.

Thank you to the many families who have shared their stories and ideas with us. Names and even some details have been changed, and some stories were combined to disguise the families involved. The stories told and sent to us have enriched our lives and our understanding of ways to make honor work in families.

Thank you to Dr. Skip Truscott and Dr. Ted Moore for your evaluation and suggestions for chapter 8 regarding teen brain development.

How to use this book

This book has been designed for use in a number of contexts. Not only will you be able to read and learn about honor yourself, but you can also work through this book with others.

In small groups or a Sunday school class, assign chapters to be read in advance and have people answer the questions at the end of each chapter. When you meet together, discuss the chapter and the answers, looking for ways to apply the material to family situations.

An appendix is also included at the end of the book, containing eight Family Together Times. These practical, interactive discussion sessions will take approximately twenty minutes and are for families with children between the ages of two and eighteen. They are intended to help your family learn what the Scriptures teach about honor and to show you ways to apply the principles presented in this book.

ONE

You'll Never be
the Same

It's fun to listen to new parents talk about their babies. At the three-month reunion of a childbirth class, you might hear:

"Look at Rachel's long fingers. I'll bet she'll play the piano."

"This boy's going to be a great baseball player someday."

"We're going to make some changes in our family. No TV for this kid. Only good reading."

"Yeah, we're getting rid of all the junk food in our house. Anthony is going to grow up healthy."

"Jay and I want to have lots of children so Caleb will always have someone to play with."

High hopes and idealistic goals are a part of every young family. New moms and dads look at their little bundles of joy and envision a family where cooperation reigns over self-centeredness, closeness overcomes competitiveness, and a joy-filled family is the inevitable result.

An interesting transition takes place in many parents, however, as their families grow and mature. These same parents give up their positive vision in exchange for basic survival skills. They just want to get through the day. They can hardly wait for their child to go to kindergarten or graduate from high school and be out of the house.

As parents gain experience in the work of parenting, their attitudes seem to change:

First baby: At the first sign of distress—a whimper, a frown— you pick up the baby.

Second baby: You pick up your baby when her wails threaten to wake up your firstborn.

Third baby: You teach your three-year-old how to rewind the mechanical swing.

First baby: You prewash your newborn's clothes, color-coordinate them, and fold them neatly in the little bureau.

Second baby: You check to make sure the clothes are clean and discard only those with the darkest stains.

Third baby: Boys can wear pink, can't they?

First baby: You take your infant to Baby Gymnastics, Baby Swim, and Baby Story Hour.

Second baby: You take your infant to a co-op play group.

Third baby: You take your infant to the supermarket and the dry cleaners.

First baby: The first time you leave your baby with a sitter you call home five times.

Second baby: Just before you walk out the door, you remember to leave a number where you can be reached.

Third baby: You leave instructions for the sitter to call only if she sees blood.

First baby: You spend a good bit of every day just gazing at the baby.

Second baby: You spend a bit of every day watching to be sure your older child isn't squeezing, poking, or hitting the baby.

Third baby: You spend a little bit of each day hiding from the children.

These situations are funny because there's some truth in them. We have dreams, goals, and expectations for our families. Some are subconscious, and others are written in our daily planners. Parents want to give their children an equal or better experience than they had. They want to help their children to be smart or athletic or independent. They want to have a family that functions as a team and provides friendships for each other.

WHY is it then that eager, hopeful parents turn into frustrated, disillusioned parents in just a few years?

Why is it then that eager, hopeful parents turn into frustrated, disillusioned parents in just a few years?

The same childbirth class that sounded so hopeful at its three-month reunion might sound like this ten years later:

"I wish I could get Rachel and Devin to pick up after themselves without grumbling. Nothing seems to work."

"Anthony's the same way. He gets angry when I ask him to do anything."

"We've got a real problem with arguing, and I don't know what to do about it."

"Our kids bicker all the time. We've tried everything. I'm about ready to give them boxing gloves and start charging admission!"

every child is unique

Parents hunger for answers. Too often, though, we believe those answers are all about following the do-this-and-everything-will-be-fine parenting advice we keep hearing and reading about. And some of us fear that finding the answers is only half the battle. How can we possibly do everything we're supposed to do?

One of the realities of family life is that children have minds and wills of their own. Children aren't robots run by remote control. When they're young, their parents can exert quite a bit of control, setting boundaries and limits. As children grow, however, the ability to control them diminishes. Children are able to make more and more of their own decisions, often contrary to their parents' desires.

One mom of a two-year-old said, "This is a great age. My son loves to see me. It's easy for me to make him laugh. He comes running to me with his arms spread out. He wants to be with me, and

I feel loved and appreciated." That's a far cry from the mom of an eight-year-old who said, "I feel as though we're in a constant tug of war. Whenever I ask my son to do anything, I get resistance."

Even the best parenting tips won't guarantee that children will make right choices. God has given each person a will. The same child who chooses to obey with a good attitude has the potential to pout at every instruction. An older sister can be kind and helpful with Mom and then turn around and be mean to her younger brother.

Furthermore, each child is unique. Every parent of more than one child sees the differences between them. One may be hyperactive while another is calm and quiet. A brother likes to talk non-stop while his sister hardly says a word. One child is easygoing while another struggles with angry outbursts. Some children have obsessive-compulsive tendencies, and others struggle with problems like Attention Deficit Disorder (ADD) and impulsivity. For genetic reasons, some children even have a predisposition to alcoholism, criminal behavior, or mental illness.

Parents need real answers. It seems that many parenting books have been written by authors who have compliant children. They believe that by following a few steps, children will turn out great. Unfortunately, many parents find these books superficial, lacking the depth needed to provide significant change in their families.

Parenting is not easy. Even Adam and Eve, the first man and woman, disobeyed, and God had to discipline them. Jesus called twelve disciples, yet one of them chose to betray him. The children of Israel continually whined, complained, and rebelled against God. He faithfully disciplined them and called them back to make the right choices. Even perfect parenting doesn't produce perfect children.

God designed the family as the place where children learn and grow. That means that imperfect parents are the teachers. That's scary. In fact, many parents feel guilty because of their children's poor choices. "If I had only done things differently," they say. These parents realize the tremendous influence they have on their children.

God has given us answers in his Word, the Bible. All of us parents need the daily grace, mercy, and forgiveness that God offers. On the one hand, we shouldn't riddle ourselves with guilt because of past failures, yet on the other we can't let our imperfection be an excuse to stop growing and learning. Although parents can't ultimately determine the outcome of their children, they do have a tremendous influence on them. Some families do better than others, leading us to conclude that there are some secrets or principles that work. Over the years in our own families, as well as in our counseling and teaching of others, we've found honor to be an amazing principle with many ramifications for family life.

HoNor to the Rescue

This is a book about honor. Honor doesn't just address behavior. It involves the heart. Too often, parents focus only on getting the right actions. But behavior change is not enough. Honor deals with deeper issues in family life. As families practice honor, they experience great rewards. Some children are harder to parent than others. Each child is different, and motivating each one to make appropriate changes can be a lifelong challenge. We've discovered that honor is an excellent and refreshing way to motivate children, enhance family life, and bring closeness to relationships.

---

for every form of selfishness in a family, there is an honor-based solution.

Mr. Porter was a middle-school history teacher. He'd met a lot of students, but one year a boy named Matt stood out. Matt was a good student and a local paper carrier. He was responsible and well liked by others, and he seemed to be a wonderful example of success. Mr. Porter wanted to know why.

"I don't know," Matt told him. "I'm just like all my brothers and sisters." There were eight children in Matt's family. This intrigued Mr. Porter all the more, so he said, "Could I come home and meet your family?"

Later that week, Matt took Mr. Porter home. As Mr. Porter watched Matt's family interact, he began to notice that something was special about them. The children seemed happy. Love, unity, and cooperation filled the home.

Mr. Porter said to Matt, "Explain this to me. You don't have all the things that everybody else has, and yet you're happy. To what do you attribute your success?"

"I don't know...unless it's honor."

"Honor? What do you mean?"

"Ever since we were young, my parents have emphasized honor in our home." Later Mr. Porter talked with Matt's dad. "Tell me more about honor in your family."

"Families are made up of imperfect people," he began. "From infants to adults, each person has a tendency to make selfish choices. We've learned, though, that for every form of selfishness in a family there's an honor-based solution. Honor thinks of what would please someone else and gives more than is expected. It's putting someone else's needs above your own. Honor values others in tangible ways. Children can learn honor and so can parents. Sure, confrontation is still necessary, and discipline still takes work. But we've found that when we focus on developing honor, we see amazing results."

That visit made a marked impression on Mr. Porter. Something special was going on in that home. Matt's parents weren't able to buy their children the finer things in life or allow them to participate in the latest fad, but they were able to give them something even more valuable—a sense of family honor. Each member of that family learned to value the others and enjoy them. That strengthened the family as a whole, and it also helped each individual to be successful in life.

After studying and working with hundreds of families, we've come to understand why some fare much better than others. Success is more than just having two cars, a nice house, a dog, and two children. It has to do with character development and how equipped family members are to relate to others outside the family. It involves creating homes where children and adults are able to make mistakes and learn from them, to grow spiritually, emotionally, and relationally with each other. Even families that have broken apart or suffered significant wounds can develop the qualities necessary to be successful. Single-parent families, blended families, and reconstructed families are all finding real solutions through honor.

HoNor is a gift

When we conduct honor workshops, we like to invite someone up to receive a gift. We tell the audience, "Showing honor is like giving a gift. We want to give a gift to someone here to help everyone remember this concept. In fact," we continue, "you can tell that a person appreciates the gift by the facial expression. The same is true when we honor others. People appreciate it, and you can see it on their faces."

At this point, we give a gift to our volunteer and everyone watches that person open it. To the surprise of our guest, the gift is a small plastic bag full of dirt. We then tell our audience, "Many times we treat each other in dishonoring ways, and it's like giving dirt to them."

Then we pull out a second gift. We tell our volunteer that we didn't want to be remembered by a gift of dirt, so we've decided to give a real gift as well. Inside this wrapping paper, the volunteer finds two candy bars, one to keep and one to give away to show honor to someone else.

You can use this activity in your family to illustrate a valuable lesson about relationships. We all wish we could receive a gift, but instead we sometimes receive hurtful words. It's like receiving dirt. This visual illustration helps people think about the way they treat others. It's one way to motivate family members to consider honor in their relationships.

take it a step further

1. List as many phrases as you can that contain the word *honor* (for example, honor student, Your Honor, etc.) Can you think of ten? What do these different uses reveal about the word *honor* and its meaning?

2. In Mark 6:4, Jesus gives an example of a time when honor isn't present in a family. What do you think Jesus is saying? You may want to use a Bible commentary to help explain your answer. What does this say about families in general?

3. Consider the statement, "For every form of selfishness in a family, there's an honor-based solution." How might honor help the following three problems in family life: complaining, children arguing, and parents yelling at children?

4. What is an improper use of honor according to James 2:1-4?

Honor changes people

Honor changes the way people think, the way we act, and the way we treat others. Honor motivates us as parents to treat our children differently. It gives children more constructive ways to interact with their parents. It helps siblings develop tolerance and patience. Honor builds a strong bond that, in turn, benefits all members of the family.

Honor adds that little bit of grace that transforms family life. It focuses on others and produces stronger relationships. It's not as concerned with protecting a reputation as it is with doing what's right. Honor is motivating and contagious and treats individuals as special. It brings joy to others but has a special reward for those who give it. Honor is like the oil in a machine, making it possible for the job to get done with less friction and less conflict.

If you simplified the definition of *honor,* it might look like this:

Honor	Treating people as special,
	doing more than what's expected,
	and having a good attitude

Consider the experience of Kathleen McDonald, a single mom, and her four-year-old daughter, Jill. Jill had a problem with complaining: "I can't find my jump rope," "I'm bored," "Nobody wants to play with me," "I don't want this sandwich," and on and on. Kathleen also developed a bad habit of nagging: "You're going to be late," "Close your mouth when you eat," "Your shirt's not tucked in."

Kathleen didn't like what she saw in herself. "I focused so much on my daughter's complaining that I didn't realize how much I nagged. Seeing our negative patterns discouraged me. I began to make changes, though, and became more honoring." She set limits for Jill, gave firm instructions, and followed through. As a result, Kathleen was able to stop nagging. "I was then able to show Jill how to honor me in return. I explained to her that complaining is dishonoring and that no one wants to listen to that kind of moaning and groaning. I taught Jill how to talk about problems in a more constructive way. Honor's done a tremendous amount for our relationship."

Honor is desperately Needed

Parents may think that the negative behavior they see in their children is simply a stage they'll grow out of. Unfortunately, instead of growing out of bad patterns, children actually grow into them. If not counteracted, selfish habits will simply become more entrenched.

Of course, children are not the only ones who struggle with selfishness. Parents are often surprised by their own selfish tendencies. One dad put it this way: "I used to think I was a pretty righteous person. Then I got married. That required sacrifice and revealed a lot of my own selfishness. But that was nothing compared to having kids! I now wrestle with selfishness on a much larger scale!" When self-centeredness increases, it's no wonder that certain behaviors like yelling, arguing, teasing, defiance, bad attitudes, bickering, and anger become a lifestyle. Unchecked selfishness creates multiple problems, resulting in tension and distance in relationships.

God knew that selfishness would hinder relationships, so he provided honor as the solution. Romans 12:10 says, "Honor one another above yourselves." Honor counteracts selfishness in a family, and it does it in a positive way. Instead of continual criticism and "Don't do that!" statements, honor gives families a vision for unselfishness. Individuals learn healthier skills for relating and find more wholesome ways of expressing themselves.

In John Sawyer's family, sons Ross, fourteen, and Derick, twelve, bickered continually. Car rides and mealtimes were the battlegrounds for vicious arguments. John and his wife, Karen, were disheartened by the tension in their home and decided to make some changes.

First, the couple made a list of the specific negative things they heard Ross and Derick say to each other. Then they sat down with each of the boys individually and discussed the problem. John and Karen offered positive alternatives and promised to point out the arguing and bickering every time they heard it. The offender would then have to stop, pause, and rephrase his comment in an honoring way. Although it took lots of work and much time, the Sawyer family began to make significant changes. Most importantly, Dad and Mom targeted their discipline in productive ways. "I'm amazed at the dramatic changes we've seen in our home since we've focused on honor," John says.

Why is family Life so complicated?

As the years pass, family relationships become more complicated. Parents may then give up and settle for just going through the motions of parenting. One mom said, "Three things are on my to-do list each day: Get up, survive, and go to bed." Some parents have lost their joy. Their positive vision for family life has evaporated.

Some parents have lost their joy.

Here's what's happening behind the scenes. As families grow, the number of relationships grows as well—and not in a one-to-one ratio. With just a husband and a wife, there are two relationships, husband to wife and wife to husband. But with the arrival of just one child, the number of relationships increases to six: Dad to Mom, Mom to Dad, Dad to child, child to Dad, Mom to child, and child to Mom. When a second child enters the picture, the number of relationships jumps from six to twelve.

Carrie and I (Scott) adopted our twins, Megan and Elizabeth, when they were four years old. At that time, our family already included five people. Megan and Elizabeth brought our total to seven people and increased the number of family relationships from twenty to forty-two overnight. Forty-two different patterns of relating were going on at the same time, an awesome thing to realize, let alone try to manage.

Reality hit at one of our first meals together. Carrie planned a "make your own taco" dinner. She prepared several ingredients and placed them on the table for everyone to make his or her own meal. I sat at one end of the table, Carrie was at the other end, and we had ten different ingredients and five children between us. We thanked God for the food, and the amen seemed to be the starting buzzer for some kind of mad scramble. Each child wanted a different ingredient from somewhere else on the table. Carrie and I both stood up and tried to help them all get what they wanted. After several minutes of mayhem, we looked at each other, exasperated, and Carrie said, "I guess this is the last time we have this meal for a while!"

Things were similar for Diane Barclay and her family. When the children were younger, the family enjoyed many special times together. When the children got older, however, Diane and her husband began to feel like taxi drivers going in different directions to take children to all their activities. The family rarely ate dinner together, and quality time, if you could call it that, happened in the car. "My family was pulled in so many different directions, we were drifting apart," Diane says. "It seemed as if we didn't know each other anymore."

These parents realized that changes needed to occur for the family to be close again. They used honor to explain to their children the importance of setting aside Sunday dinner and a family night each week. Diane says, "Now that I see the importance of honor, things are different. It's changed the way we plan our schedules and the activities we choose. We're enjoying our family more, and we've grown closer together."

AN IMPORTANT DISTINCTION

When families think about honor, they often restrict their thinking to respectful behavior—being polite, courteous, and having good manners. This is a narrow understanding and is only a small portion of what honor actually is. Respectful behavior, although a subset of honor, is incomplete by itself. For example, Susie learned manners at an early age. "What a nice girl," people said. Susie learned acceptable behavior, but as she got older she rebelled against the rules, finding them empty and overly restrictive. Teaching respect is not enough.

The difference between respect and honor is not simply semantics.

The difference between *respect* and *honor* is not simply semantics. As with most synonyms, there are important differences between the two words. The Greek words used in the New Testament illustrate the difference between *respect* and *honor*. The Greek word often translated "respect" is *phobos,* from which we get the English word *phobia.* At its root, it means "to fear." Respect is outward, focusing on a person's position or on the power of an office. People respect police officers or judges because of their authoritative position. When only respect is emphasized in family life, it leads to outer conformity, false intimacy, and, eventually, distant relationships.

The Greek word that is often translated "honor" in the New

Testament comes from *timae,* which means "worth" or "value." It's one thing to respect (fear) God because of his tremendous power and greatness and another thing to honor (value) him because of those qualities. Worshipers give God glory and honor and praise because they value him.

It is one thing to obey a crossing guard out of respect for the position. It is yet another to show honor to that crossing guard because of friendship.

- Respect acknowledges a person's position; honor attaches worth to that person as an individual.
- Respect teaches manners and proper behavior in the presence of others; honor teaches an appreciation of that person.
- Respect can become a technique to make a family look good on the outside; honor builds the hidden bonds that provide strength and lasting unity.

Both honor and respect have their place. When children are young, they learn respectful behavior. As they grow older, they can develop a heart response of honor as well. It's good to teach respectful behavior, but it's important not to stop there. Honor adds a deeper dimension to relationships.

When families catch a vision for honor, they begin to think differently. The dad who gets up in the morning and sees his son's underwear on the bathroom floor again stops to think before he starts yelling. *How can I respond with honor here?* he asks himself. Yelling is not very honoring. A teenager begins to see that disrespect and sarcasm don't feel right anymore. Those methods of communication aren't consistent with who she is now. She has learned honor, the ability to value others for who they are. As individuals learn to honor one another, they begin to see life differently. Every situation is now an opportunity to value others. Honor and dishonor begin to stand out, and we choose our actions and responses more carefully.

The Rivera family has worked hard to develop a sense of family honor.

> We teach our children that being a Rivera is special. We're not just out for ourselves. We work as a team. When a job needs to be done, the Rivera Team pulls together. We work hard to clean up the house, or plant a garden, or do yard work. We also have special privileges as a family, going out to eat, playing games, or having ice cream together. We treat each other as special. Meanness is not acceptable because it doesn't fit our identity. Angry outbursts require an apology because hurtful words aren't consistent with the idea that we value each other.

Honor changes *how* families interact. Emotions are handled differently. The family develops new conflict-management skills. Teasing and joking are limited. The family becomes a place where people value each other and appreciate strengths. When individuals show weaknesses, they receive encouragement instead of ridicule or harsh criticism. Honor teaches us to view our families differently. We just can't live those old ways anymore. We've learned that each person has value and that we all do better and enjoy life more when honor is demonstrated.

Honor goes deeper

Parents who only focus on behavior change are devastated when their children reveal unresolved issues of the heart as they grow older. The child who steals the family car, the unmarried teenager who gets pregnant, or the boy who starts using drugs all have one thing in common: a heart problem that's developed over time. The heart consists of thoughts, intentions, motivations, desires, and fantasies.

My husband and I (Joanne) keep a growth chart on the wall in our home. The boys love to see how tall they've grown from year to year. But height isn't the most important measurement of growth. The real measurement of a person is to put a tape around his heart.

A preschool teacher told a little boy to sit down. He refused. The teacher, not wanting to be outdone, leaned over and said sternly, "You sit down!" The boy sat down, looked up at the teacher, and replied, "I'm sitting on the outside, but I'm standing on the inside." Too many children are like that, changing their behavior in response to discipline but continuing to disobey in their hearts.

Many parents discipline with a two-step process. It might look like Figure 1. Parents see wrong behavior and then use a number of

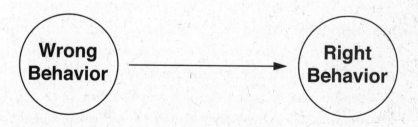

Figure 1. How most misbehavior is handled by parents

techniques to get their child to do what's right. When the child does the right behavior, parents believe the discipline is complete and they've done their job. Behavior is changed, but the heart isn't.

A good discipline process requires four steps and would look like Figure 2. First, identify the wrong behavior. For example, your daughter begins to complain when you ask her to help with the dishes.

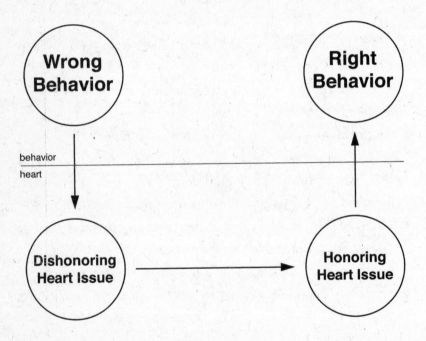

Figure 2. How misbehavior is handled with honor

Second, identify the dishonoring heart issue. Maybe she has a problem with anger or doesn't handle instructions well.

Third, identify the honoring heart issue. Perhaps she could develop flexibility, giving a few minutes to be helpful.

Fourth, the right behavior grows out of the honoring heart issue. She could help with the dishes without complaining or respectfully discuss an alternative.

The goal of discipline is to help children not only act correctly, but also to think correctly and to become the people God made them to be. Honor addresses what's going on below the surface and considers a child's heart. Jesus criticized the Pharisees and teachers of the law for their hypocrisy: "You clean the outside of the cup and dish, but inside they are full of greed and self-indulgence.... First clean the inside of the cup and dish, and then the outside also will be clean" (Matthew 23:25-26). When you teach children to change their hearts, you will see them make attitude adjustments, not just behavioral changes. You'll get to the root of disobedience or immaturity, and you'll help your children make lifelong changes.

take it a step further

1. Look up *honor* and *respect* in a dictionary. How are they similar? How are they different?

2. Both *phobos* (respect) and *timae* (honor) are used in Romans 13:7. What is being said in this verse about esteeming others?

3. Compare the idea of fearing God (1 Peter 2:17) and honoring God (Revelation 4:11). In light of this chapter, what is being emphasized in each of these verses?

4. What does the concept of honor add to a family that has only emphasized respect?

5. Identify one way you could be more honoring in your family.

THREE

More than just following directions

One day a dad was out in the woods and kicked over a bottle. Immediately a genie popped out and offered him one wish. Thinking hard, the dad got out a map and, looking it over, decided to ask for peace in the Middle East.

"Well, that's very hard," said the genie. "There hasn't been peace in the Middle East for many years."

The dad paused for a moment and then brightened with a thought. He turned to the genie and said, "Well, then, maybe you could just do something to teach my children to show honor to my wife and me."

The genie paused for a moment, then thoughtfully said, "Let me look at that map again."

Most parents recognize the value of teaching their children how to obey, but few teach their children honor. Honor and obedience differ in several ways.

HONOR	Treating people as special, doing more than what's expected, and having a good attitude

obedience   Doing what someone says,

right away,

without being reminded

God knew what he was doing when he gave these two instructions to children in Ephesians 6:1-3: "Children, obey your parents in the Lord, for this is right. 'Honor your father and mother'—which is the first commandment with a promise—'that it may go well with you and that you may enjoy long life on the earth.'" If children learn obedience and honor, they also develop the qualities needed to be successful adults.

When children develop obedience, they learn to do a task without being reminded. They learn how to report back, do work they might rather not do, follow directions, and complete a job without being watched. They learn responsibility, a willingness to serve, and faithfulness to do a good job.

Honor also has several skills hidden within it. Having a good attitude, doing more than what's expected, seeing what needs to be done and doing it without being asked, encouraging others, and contributing to a nurturing atmosphere—all are learned through honor.

---

if you want your children to fly straight, teach them obedience. if you want them to fly high, teach them honor.

Both obedience and honor are important. When children learn obedience and honor, they develop skills that will make them successful in life. If you want your children to fly straight, teach them obedience. If you want them to fly high, teach them honor.

obedieNce iʃ ʃouNdatioNal

Ephesians 6:1 says, "Children, obey your parents in the Lord, for this is right." The words *this is right* are very important. When children do what's right, they experience a feeling of satisfaction, a freedom from fear of being caught or punished. Doing what's right enables a child to have a clear conscience. Some children don't have that feeling of freedom. In fact, these children live with guilt because of disobedience.

Others experience a continual tension because they know in the back of their minds that there's something they haven't done that they should have. One girl we'll call Shelly felt that her parents were always looking for more things for her to do. She didn't have a feeling of freedom. It turned out, though, that Shelly had a problem completing tasks and doing what was asked. She didn't make her bed or finish her homework, she left the bathroom a mess, and she forgot to practice her flute. These were all things she was supposed to do.

Shelly's parents saw that she wasn't obeying, but they realized that they were part of the problem. They hadn't made their expectations clear. When both Shelly and her parents clarified expectations, and she did what they asked, she felt a freedom in her spirit that said, "I've completed what I needed to do."

When we teach this concept to teens, we ask them to describe how they feel on Friday when school's out and they have no homework for the weekend. They feel relief and freedom. It's the same way you, as an adult, might feel on Friday afternoon when work is over and you don't have to take projects home for the weekend. Children can feel that sense of freedom every day by obeying their parents and completing the work they've been asked to do.

Like Shelly's parents, however, we have to be clear about what we expect from our children. One family made a project checklist for their sixteen-year-old son. At first, the son thought the list was childish. But it helped to clarify expectations for both the parents and the teen: "When you get these things checked off, you're free." The teen quickly saw that he hadn't been doing the things that his parents had asked him to do, but he now decided to work hard and get them done. Parents and son all experienced greater satisfaction and peace.

Sometimes children become frustrated because they've done what's expected, but then their parents add more work without considering their plans or desires. It's as if the reward for doing a good job is receiving more work. This makes learning obedience more difficult. Both children and parents benefit from clarifying the expectations up front.

Obedience requires submission on the part of a child. Words like submission and obedience often have a negative connotation in our culture because of some who have abused their authority. Abuse of authority is wrong, but its occurrence doesn't justify disobedience.

Honor Makes it All Work Smoothly

Ephesians 6:2-3 reveals additional benefits for the child who learns to show honor. "'Honor your father and mother'—which is the first commandment with a promise—'that it may go well with you and that you may enjoy long life on the earth.'" Honor provides a foundation for children that sets them up to be happy, joyful, and to enjoy life.

From the time children are very young, they need to learn what honor is and why it's important. Scripture says, "Honor your father and mother" eight times. Why? Because God knows that there is a tendency to do the opposite, to forget the value of Mom or Dad.

Although obedience gets the job done, honor addresses *how* the job is done. Honor keeps the family running smoothly. It brings joy to the giver as well as to the receiver. But honoring others doesn't come naturally. It needs to be taught.

Consider Wendy and her teenage son, Tom. Being a single mom, Wendy needed help around the house, and her fourteen-year-old son was certainly capable of doing some of the work.

"Tom, I'm frustrated about the chores you're supposed to do."

"What's the problem? I do everything you tell me to do."

"I know, but that's just the point. I always have to tell you to do your chores. I have to tell you when the trash is full and needs to be taken out. You leave messes around the house and expect me to clean them up—like dirty glasses and plates—and a sticky counter after you fix yourself a snack."

Wendy was frustrated, but the problem wasn't obedience. Tom

was obeying. He was doing the jobs when Mom asked, but she wanted more than that. She felt as if she were being taken advantage of. Wendy realized that not only did the constant need for reminders bother her, but it also demonstrated an area of weakness in her son. Tom needed to learn honor.

Honor requires us to ask different questions about life.

Honor requires a shift in our thinking. It requires us to ask different questions about life. It means acting and talking in a manner that pleases others, even when they are not around. Honor teaches you to consider the needs of others, not just your own.

It took several weeks of teaching and illustrating honor before Tom really understood. Eventually, Wendy saw improvement at school and other situations outside the home. Over time, Tom caught a vision for honor at home as well. This resulted in joy for both Tom and his mother.

Let's look at it another way. When you're employed, you're usually given a job description. It clarifies your responsibilities and your tasks. You look at that description, and you know what you're supposed to be working on. Ephesians 6:1-3 gives a job description for children. They have an assignment to work on while they're young, and the reward is outlined for them. Obedience and honor are the job. A clear conscience and an enjoyable life are the rewards.

Honor Addresses Whining and Complaining

One problem that children often face is the challenge of obeying and showing honor when they don't like what they've been asked to do. When unhappy with an instruction or a no answer, some children whine.

This is no news flash: Whining and complaining are manipulative techniques used by children to get what they want. Children must see that their tricks don't work. They need to learn a more honoring way to communicate.

Another technique children often use is badgering. One little boy was overheard telling another, "If you want a kitten, start by asking for a horse." Children continually fire a barrage of questions or complaints at parents in order to wear them down so that, eventually, they'll give in. Why do children do it? Because it works. Point out these behaviors as tricks and refuse to play the game. Instead, teach your children honoring ways to ask permission, make requests, and get approval.

Some parents wonder if it's ever okay to allow children to question their instructions. Should you always require prompt obedience? Should you talk about instructions with your children? These are important questions. Obedience can be complicated. Even adults can have problems submitting to authority. What do you do if you don't agree with what your boss or landlord says? What's a godly response to authority?

Even young children need to know how to handle their feelings when they disagree with someone who has given them an instruction. It's important to address the difficult question, "How do I obey when I don't feel like it?" Teaching children how to respond will help them tremendously as they get older. Children have two choices when they don't agree or they don't want to obey.

"Obey First, and Then We'll Talk About It"

One of the problems with obedience is that children often don't want to comply. They have their own agenda. Parents, of course, want to value their children's ideas and wishes. We want them to be able to make their own decisions and to be happy. But it's also important for children to learn to give up their agendas and follow instructions—even when they don't want to. Too many parents have ended up with children who won't follow the simplest instructions without discussing it. Sending the message, "Obey first, and then we'll talk about it" emphasizes obedience.

If little Brian has pulled a chair over to the counter and is climbing onto it, you might say, "Brian, we don't climb on chairs."

"But I was just…"

"No, you need to get down. Obey first, and then we'll talk about it." Once he gets down, discuss the problem and find a solution together.

Or consider this dialogue: "Karl, it's time to get your pajamas on."

"But I'm not tired. I don't want to go to bed yet."

"Put your pajamas on, and then we'll talk about it."

And what if this approach still doesn't result in obedience? Children who haven't learned how to obey should be given fewer choices. If you tell your daughter to go pick out something to wear and get dressed, but she dawdles or starts playing, you may say, "You have wasted too much time. I'm going to pick out your clothes for you."

Parents, in an attempt to honor their children, often make the mistake of justifying the instruction before the child obeys. They believe the child has a right to understand why the request is being made and to talk about it. No parents want their children to fall into a pattern of blindly following a leader's instructions, but evaluating is an advanced skill. Many parents have reacted to authoritarianism and ended up with children who cannot follow instructions without a dialogue. These children make poor employees, develop selfish attitudes about following someone else's leadership, and have a difficult time in relationships—all because they haven't learned how to sacrifice their own agenda for others.

Think about this approach in light of your spiritual life. Sometimes God asks his people to obey even when they don't understand why. In Genesis 22, Abraham was told to sacrifice his son Isaac without understanding why God would make such a request. Abraham's obedience was an act of faith, and God rewarded him. In Acts 8:26-39, Philip was told to leave Samaria, where a revival was taking place, and go to the desert. When he went there, he discovered the Ethiopian man who was ready to trust Christ. In Acts 10, Peter went to Cornelius's house without knowing why, only to discover that God wanted to bring salvation to the Gentiles. Obedience does not have to hinge on understanding why.

Discussing an instruction can also give children the wrong impression about obedience—that if they don't like the request they have just cause to resist. The fact is, many times we adults have to obey even if we don't like it or it's not convenient. Once children learn this skill, they can advance to another technique that evaluates the instruction and offers a creative alternative.

The Wise Appeal

Privilege and responsibility go together. When children learn to be responsible and follow directions without arguing or complaining, they're ready for the privilege of the wise appeal. This technique helps children address their own feelings and still respond in an honoring way.

Let's look at a typical example. Fifteen-year-old Cal comes home from school at 3:00 P.M., plops his books down, and says to himself, "Whew! I'm tired. I just want to listen to my CDs and rest."

Just then, his mom, Janet, comes in to greet him. "Cal, I'm glad you're home from school. I'd like you to go out and mow the lawn."

Here's one way this scene could play itself out. Cal looks up at his mother and, irritated, says, "Mom! Mow the lawn? Not now!"

Janet gets more intense, willing to take on the challenge. "Listen. I don't need an argument. I don't make you do many things around this house. But you need to go out and mow the lawn now!"

Did you see what happened? Janet became more entrenched in her position and came on stronger. Could Cal have responded in a way that might have influenced his mom differently? Let's rewind that tape and try it again, this time illustrating a more honoring way for Cal to respond.

"Cal, I'm glad you're home from school," Janet says. "I'd like you to go out and mow the lawn."

Cal is silent for a moment, trying to deal with his emotions. "Mom, I understand you want me to mow the grass because it's getting high. I have a problem with that because I'm tired right now. I didn't get much sleep last night, and I had a tough day at school. I was counting on resting and listening to my music for a while. Could I please mow the lawn in two hours?"

Janet thinks for a moment and then replies, "That sounds fine. I'd just like to have it done before dinner."

Maybe you're thinking, "My kids won't do that. It sounds like a cross between *The Brady Bunch* and *Leave It to Beaver.*"

Your children can learn this because it's actually a formula.

---

the Wise Appeal says:

"I understand that you want me to…because…"

"I have a problem with that because…"

"Could I please…?"

Even parents with preschoolers can teach the wise appeal to their children. The parent can coach the child by saying, "I understand that you want me to…," and allowing the child to fill in the blanks. A young child may say, "I don't know what you want me to do" or "I don't have an alternative." Say, "That's part of the wise appeal. Why don't you ask me some questions so you understand what I'm asking you to do." Or, "In order to have a wise appeal, you need to think of a creative idea that helps both of us come to a better solution." It's amazing what happens when children grasp this idea. As they get older, they grow into the wise appeal and learn a valuable skill.

Let's rewind the story one more time and take apart this wise appeal in order to understand why it's so valuable.

"Mom, I understand you want me to mow the grass because it's getting high." Cal demonstrates honor by expressing his understanding of his mother's desire. This is very important. When parents feel understood, they're more likely to listen to alternatives, negotiate, or compromise.

"I have a problem with that because I'm tired right now. I didn't get much sleep last night, and I had a tough day at school. I was counting on resting and listening to my music for a while." The second step in the wise appeal helps the parent understand the child. Here, Janet learns more about Cal's situation. When parents understand a child's predicament, they're more likely to be accommodating.

"Could I please mow the lawn in two hours?" The third part of the wise appeal is honoring because it gives a creative alternative. The child focuses on a solution, not just the problem; the parent hears a suggestion, not just a complaint. Now the child is working with the parent toward a common goal. When your child appeals to you in this honoring way, you're more likely to allow for an alternative.

If a young child continues to whine after you've said no, you might say, "I've already said no. If you'd like to appeal, I'll listen. But if you continue to whine, you'll have to go sit on your bed."

The wise appeal is an important skill to teach your children. Children need to know how to appeal in an honoring way when they don't agree. After all, sometimes parents don't have all the facts.

If you tell your daughter to get into the car because it's time to leave, but she has to go to the bathroom, you don't want her to "obey first, and then we'll talk about it" or you'll be driving down the road looking for a public rest room. It's important to give children an honoring way to communicate when they have a problem with the instructions they've been given.

When I (Joanne) taught my son, Timothy, the wise appeal, he was just a preschooler. I remember one afternoon when he was four years old. He was in the backyard playing, and I called to him to come into the house. Tim came over and said, "I really know you want me to come in, but I really want to stay outside. Could I please play a little longer?" This was a four-year-old version of the wise appeal. Tim was getting the idea. He came to me to talk about the problem instead of just whining, "Not yet." Even young children can learn this skill and graciously appeal when they are unhappy with an instruction.

After you've taught the wise appeal, you may say to your seven-year-old son, "It's time to clean up the playroom now. We have to run errands." If he's just become involved in his train set, he might say, "I understand you want me to clean up the toys because we have to go out. I have a problem with that because I just set up my train track. Could I please leave my train out until we get home?"

Of course, a child in this situation needs to be able to accept no as an answer. A child who is unable to accept no must go back to "obey first, and then we'll talk about it." When a child learns how to obey with a good attitude, then the wise appeal can be used with discretion.

At first the wise appeal may sound unrealistic. One mom came to us and said, "I didn't think the wise appeal would work with my nine-year-old son. But a couple of weeks ago I was frustrated with his whining, and I decided to try it. I taught it to him and have encouraged him to use it when he's tempted to whine and complain. He likes it. I like it too, and it's made our dialogue more pleasant. I just wanted to tell you that it worked."

The wise appeal is an adult skill. Unfortunately, many adults haven't learned how to use it. Instead, they resort to complaining and passive resistance. The wise appeal helps people become part of the solution, not just complain about the problem.

Some children may try to use the wise appeal in a manipulative way, or they may not be mature enough to handle it. Cal, for example, might forget to do the lawn in two hours or might even try to use the wise appeal to get out of mowing the lawn altogether. This is unacceptable. The wise appeal results in a contract between parent and child. This contract requires trust. When a child proves to be responsible, then the child earns the privilege of more trust. Those who are not responsible enough to handle the wise appeal lose the privilege of using it for a while. Privilege and responsibility go together.

The wise appeal is illustrated in Scripture with people like Daniel (1:8-16), Nehemiah (2:1-8), and Esther (4–7). Each had a problem and had to approach those in authority in a wise way. They received positive answers to their requests, in part because of the honoring way in which their requests were made. The wise appeal is a tool that can be used by children and adults alike.

Mr. Clancy came home from work with some bad news. "What's wrong, Dad?" his daughter Sarah asked.

"I found out that I'm scheduled to work next Thursday night, and I'm going to have to miss your recital."

"Did you try the wise appeal?" asked Sarah. Their family had learned the wise appeal just a couple of months before, and Sarah had been using it with her parents.

"Uh...no," Mr. Clancy admitted, trying to hide his smile. "I don't think Mr. Baldwin would be interested in a wise appeal."

"It can't hurt," persisted Sarah. "All he can do is say no."

The next evening, Mr. Clancy came home beaming. "You're not going to believe this," he said. "I went to Mr. Baldwin and told him that I knew changing the schedule was difficult. I explained that you have a piano recital and asked if I could switch with someone else. He said he'd check on it. Just before I left work, he gave me the okay."

"That's great!" said Sarah. The Clancy family discovered just how valuable the wise appeal can be.

Children should not be allowed to challenge every request, but the wise appeal is an honoring way to address a parent. You must decide which response needs to be emphasized in your family at any given time. If children are continually wanting to discuss before obeying, you might need to focus on "obey first, and then we'll talk about it." But if your family tends to emphasize strict obedience, you might want to allow for a wise appeal, teaching your children an honoring response.

If you teach the wise appeal to your children, they'll be able to use it in a variety of different contexts. This is a tool that children can use for the rest of their lives.

Honor Makes Obedience Easier

Sometimes a child will get trapped in a negative cycle, continually doing the wrong thing over and over again. Parents discipline, but the child doesn't seem quite able to break free. These cycles can last hours, days, or even weeks at a time. The parent feels as if every interaction is a tug of war as they drag their children through the various tasks of the day. The normal suggestions for parenting just don't seem to work. Addressing wrong behavior is not enough.

When you see a negative pattern developing, use honor to set a course in a different direction.

In these particularly difficult situations, parents can take a more proactive approach. When you see a negative pattern developing, use honor to set a course in a different direction. Here's a plan for helping children get out of negative cycles.

Step One: Get Some Answers

- Have the child take a piece of paper, find a quiet place to be alone, and answer one or more of the following questions before returning. These are general questions; feel free to change them to fit the situation.
- When Mom/Dad tells me to do something, I'll say…
- When Mom/Dad corrects me, I'll say…
- When I've done something wrong, I will…

- When I'm disappointed with a no answer, I will…
- When my brother/sister is annoying me, I will…
- Here are five ways I can honor others…

For younger children, you can simplify this step by asking them to focus on only one question and then talk with you about it.

Step Two: Talk About It

Have a discussion that goes something like this: "Family life has been hard lately. I know you've been having a difficult time, but I want our family to be a place where we can have fun and relax together. That happens when each family member is honoring. When one person doesn't show honor, then the whole family suffers. It doesn't just hurt you. It hinders the joy in the family. Each of us brings to this family special benefits that can only come from that person. I add things to the family that are different from anyone else. You do too. When you're doing well, our family is a joyful place, and we all appreciate your contribution. I'd like you to relate to all of us in a way that is honoring."

Step Three: Choose an Activity

Have your child choose one activity that will add to family life. "You can decorate the hall door, bake cookies, make cards for each person, look for ways to serve, or initiate a game. I'd like you to spend some time thinking about this and then report back to me when you know what you want to do."

Remember, if you choose the activity yourself and force the

child to do it, that's obedience. If the child chooses the activity and initiates it with others, that's honor.

Step Four: Help the Child Succeed

Help the child succeed with the chosen activity. It will probably take extra time on your part, but allow the child to do as much as possible. Express delight at the end and go overboard to show appreciation. Talk about joy in the family and the benefit of everyone making a contribution. End on a positive note. Even though the child may regress to negative behaviors, continue to work on it. Daily contributions may be necessary for a child to learn to give to the family. Stick with it. Honor will win in the end.

Developing honor in a family is like refinishing a valuable piece of furniture. A woman went into Tom's Refinishing Shop to get an estimate on her antique chest of drawers. After looking it over, the owner said, "We can paint it for $50 or we can stain it for $500."

"Why such a difference in price?" the customer asked.

"Some people want a quick paint job. It doesn't cost much, and it covers many of the blemishes. It looks good at first glance. But paint just deals with the surface. Staining requires that we strip the wood and fix blemishes before the stain is applied. Stain goes down deep. Even if you scratch through the surface, the stain still shows. With care and time, stain even enhances blemishes in the wood, adding personality to the furniture."

Families are like that. Some families want to look good on the outside, appearing clean and nice. Many parents, though, aren't content with the superficial. They see the need for more substantial answers and are ready to make the sacrifices necessary to help their family succeed.

take it a step further

1. Contrast the success principles found in obedience with those found in honor. Can you think of any more? How might knowing about these long-term benefits affect how you discipline your children?

2. Try to find a few more examples in the Bible of times when God asked people to "obey first, and then we'll talk about it." Try to imagine why God would ask each person to obey without fully understanding.

3. Look for additional examples of people in the Bible who used the wise appeal. What made the appeal effective in each of these situations?

4. Older children may find the wise appeal childish at first. How might a family incorporate this skill in family life without patronizing the children?

six ways to teach honor to children

Mike, at age twelve, had his first lawn-mowing job. Grandpa sat on the porch and watched him struggle with the lawn mower at the neighbor's house. Mike was determined to get the job done. At one point when Mike was taking a break, Grandpa called to him, "Hey, Mike, come over here a minute."

Mike came over and sat on the porch with his grandfather. "Let me tell you a secret," Grandpa began. "If you want to be successful and do a really good job, then look for something extra to do. Do more than what's expected. You'll be surprised at what happens."

Motivated by Grandpa's words, Mike headed back over to the neighbor's house. Instead of leaving when he was done mowing, Mike took an extra few minutes and swept the walk. He and his grandfather exchanged a warm smile. When the neighbor came out to pay Mike, he was delighted to see the extra effort. Mike's eyes widened as the neighbor paid him and then gave him a tip.

Mike learned an important lesson about honor that day. Not only did he get more money than he expected, but his positive reputation began to spread throughout the neighborhood. Most importantly, though, Mike felt good, knowing he'd done a superior job.

Honor does more than what's expected. Grandpa knew this important principle of life and shared it at a teachable moment, which made a lasting impression on his grandson.

Teaching honor is trickier than teaching obedience, since honor is a gift. It's awkward to teach someone to give you a gift. Honor must be freely given, from the heart. As parents, you can demand respect, but that just focuses on externals and doesn't get to the real issue. Honor isn't something you can demand from your children, but you can certainly motivate them to grow in it. This chapter contains six ways to help your children develop honor.

HoNor Le∬oN #1: teach children to treat people a∫ ∫pecial

Children often don't realize how specially their parents treat them. They take the daily gifts in family life for granted. Making a favorite dinner, driving to baseball games, rearranging schedules, and sacrificing other opportunities in their lives are just a few of the many things they do for their children. To help your children begin to see how honor works, occasionally say to your child with a smile, "I made you some cookies for a snack. I wanted to honor you."

---

children al∫o learn to treat people
a∫ ∫pecial when they watch how their
parent∫ treat each other.

Children also learn to treat people as special when they watch how their parents treat each other and those outside the family.

One mom came home from shopping and was greeted by her two boys.

"Ian hit me."

"Peter locked me out of the bedroom."

This was not the greeting she had hoped for, but she used this situation as an opportunity to teach her boys a lesson about honor. "How people are greeted when they come in the door is very important. The first thing they see or hear is an opportunity to show honor. I wish you'd greet me first and say something like, 'How was shopping?' or 'I'm glad you're home.'"

She and the boys decided to practice this when Dad came home that evening. They made sure the first things he heard and saw were pleasant and welcoming. When children learn honor, they think about others, not just themselves.

When dishonoring speech is expressed, use it as an opportunity to teach children how to treat others as special. Sam, age twelve, called his stepfather, Henry, at work and asked him to stop on the way home to pick up a video. Unfortunately, the movie Sam wanted wasn't available, so Henry chose a different one. When Henry arrived home, Sam was there to greet him: "Did you get my video?"

"Sorry, Sam, that one wasn't in, so I got this one instead."

"Oh, yuck, I hate that movie."

Henry paused for a moment, looked at Sam, and then said, "No problem." Henry recognized two things. First, now was not the time to launch into a lecture about gratefulness. Second, Sam had an attitude problem.

Later, Henry announced to the family, "I got a video for us to watch tonight, but Sam isn't going to watch it."

Sam said, "Hey! I changed my mind. I want to watch the video."

This was the time to deal with the problem, so Henry said, "Sam, your complaining earlier was not right. It demonstrates an ungrateful spirit. You can watch your choice of a video some other time. Tonight you'll have to find something else to do." Henry walked into his bedroom to change his clothes.

A few minutes later, Sam came in and said, "I'm sorry for complaining about the video. I'd really like to watch this one tonight." Henry sensed a repentant heart, and he chose to allow Sam to watch the video. What could have been a family squabble became an opportunity for Sam to learn how careless speech is dishonoring because it doesn't treat people as special.

Meanness is another violation of honor in family life because it's actually the opposite of treating people kindly. Habits of meanness can be hard to break in both the offender and the victim. Use a three-step approach to address this difficult issue.

First, make observations. "Mark, that was mean." "That wasn't kind, Mark." "That looks like meanness to me, Mark." These observations point out meanness, and, more importantly, they indicate that you won't tolerate it. This gives children the subtle warning that if their behavior does not change, discipline will follow.

A second step is to gently correct. "Mark, that was a mean comment. I'd like you to take a break for a few minutes in the hall and then come back to me when you're ready to talk about this." A short break can help Mark see and begin to correct mean patterns. The benefit of a break is that it's short and, in patterns like meanness, can be used several times a day without losing its effectiveness. Mark should come back after each break for a debriefing.

The third step brings honor into the picture. A child who has developed bad habits must develop good habits to replace them. "Mark, you have a habit of being mean to your brother. From now on, when you do something mean, I'm going to have you think of one kind thing to do." In addition, work with Mark at other times. Have him choose secret acts of kindness to do for various people in the family. Meanness is a violation of honor and needs to be addressed by building new habits of kindness.

Victims of meanness also need to learn honor. Too often a younger sibling will provoke an older one, encouraging a mean response that will earn the older one blame while the younger one gets off. These children aren't innocent victims. Children need to learn how to deal with meanness in life. They don't have to enter into the revenge and fighting. They can make observations, set personal boundaries, learn to get help, and avoid developing bitterness and resentment.

Treating people as special involves more than just actions. It's a way of thinking about each other. You value each person in your family and won't stoop to unkindness or put-downs. A parent's correction, comments, and responses can raise the level of honor in a family.

Honor Lesson #2: Teach Children to do More than What's Expected

I (Joanne) remember one blustery afternoon when I looked out the window and saw our trash can blowing around in the middle of the street. I called to David, age eight, who was upstairs watching a video. I asked him to please take a break from what he was doing and go out and bring the trash can in from the street before it blew away. David quickly ran outside, grabbed the can, and brought it up to the house. Then, instead of racing back to his video, he watched the trash can for a minute to see if it would blow away again. Seeing that it was still unstable, he moved it to a more secure place. I was pleased. David was being thoughtful about the intent of my instructions. That's showing honor.

Honor does more than what's expected. It looks past the words to Mom's intent. Honor involves being thoughtful and thorough about what you do.

"The bathroom is an excellent place to work on honor," one dad said. "We put up a sign by the light switch that read, 'Is the bathroom ready for the next person?' We wanted our children to turn around and look before they walked out. Hanging up the towel and picking up their dirty clothes were first on the list, but we asked each child to think of one more thing they could do to make the bathroom a little neater. They could ask questions like 'Is there toilet paper on the roller?' 'Is the sink clean?' 'Is there anything on the counter that needs to be put away?' 'Are the cupboards closed?' These are examples of ways that people can show honor, and they probably won't get any credit or reward. We then discussed Matthew 6:1-4, which talks about doing acts of righteousness in secret and receiving God's reward." Obedience does things well. Honor does them beautifully.

Honor sees the need and takes care of the problem. If it's broken, fix it. If it's empty, fill it. If it's open, shut it. If it's out, put it away. If it's messy, clean it. If you can't, then report it. That's honor.

When teaching children to do more than what's expected, parents can include honor in the instruction. You might say, "I'd like you to obey me by setting the table, then I want you to think of something extra to do to surprise me. That's showing honor. You choose; it's up to you. Report to me when you're done, and I'll check your work." Remember: If you tell them to fold the napkins in a special way, that's obedience. If they choose to add that extra touch, it's honor.

Instructing children to surprise you by doing something extra teaches them to think about your needs and desires, not just getting away with the bare minimum. When your child does some extra task, it's like giving you a gift. Receive the gift with delight. This can be a fun way to teach honor.

WHEN YOU'RE TEACHING CHILDREN WHAT HONOR
MEANS IN PRACTICAL TERMS, ATTITUDE
IS A GOOD PLACE TO START.

HONOR LESSON #3:
DEAL WITH A BAD ATTITUDE

Sometimes children obey, but they do it with a bad attitude. When you're teaching children what honor means in practical terms, attitude is a good place to start. Obedience is revealed in actions; honor is revealed in the attitude that goes along with those actions.

One dad tells the story of a time when his daughter, Marge, was seven years old.

She was yelling at her sister, so I called her upstairs to talk about it. Marge was so angry, she began yelling at me. I told her that she needed to take a break for a bit and settle down.

About a minute later she came back but was obviously not changed. Her head was tilted down, her posture was slumping, and her bottom lip was sticking out. I didn't even have to talk with her. I just told her, "I still see a problem with your attitude, Marge. I can tell you're not ready to talk with me yet. You still have a problem in your heart. I want you to go spend some more time alone until you're ready to come back with a different attitude."

This time she stayed away for about twenty minutes. When she returned, she was obviously different. In fact, I took her head in my hands and looked deep into her eyes and said, "I can see your heart in there. It looks pretty nice right now. It looks like you're ready to talk about this."

Marge giggled, and then we talked about the problem. I explained to her that she couldn't yell at her dad. I don't treat *her* that way. It's not honoring even if she's angry. We also talked about the right responses she could have when she was angry with her sister. I was able to teach Marge because I first addressed her bad attitude.

A bad attitude often comes from an angry spirit. Imagine an onion with various layers. As you peel off one layer, you see another and another, until you get to the center of the onion. Anger is like that. The most obvious signs of anger are acts of physical violence—for example, hitting, slamming things, kicking, and biting.

As children learn to control their physical reactions, the next layer becomes obvious. It involves hurtful words, such as sarcasm, teasing, and cynical remarks. They are not physical, but they are still deadly responses that parents must address. Layer after layer of angry responses can be removed until you come to a very significant one: the bad attitude. Once you reach the bad-attitude layer, you're dealing with the heart directly. A bad attitude is a form of passive resistance and shouldn't be ignored. Huffing or rolling the eyes after receiving an instruction is a symptom of a deeper problem. When a bad attitude isn't addressed, anger reveals itself in selfish, disrespectful, and mean behaviors.

Bad attitudes are generally seen in three areas—when the child receives an instruction, when the child is corrected, and when the child gets a no answer.

Don't just point out a bad attitude. Give children healthy alternatives. How should a child respond when given an instruction they'd rather not do? "Okay" is a good place to start. How should a child respond when being corrected? "I'm sorry" or "I was wrong." How should a child respond when disappointed with a no answer? "Okay, maybe next time." Honor redirects a bad attitude into constructive responses. This may sound unrealistic if your children have developed strong patterns of opposition. These suggestions, though, will get children thinking in the right direction.

If your son is angry and having a bad attitude, teach him to take a break and cool off: "Go to your room and settle down until you can talk about your anger without using your body to show it." When your son returns, talk to him about more constructive responses.

One day Mom heard some arguing in the playroom. As she listened, she determined that Gary, age eight, was telling the other children how to play a particular game. As she listened further, she realized that Gary wasn't even playing the game but was butting in to tell his friends that they were playing it the wrong way.

Mom called Gary out of the room and talked to him about what she heard. She told him that he was acting bossy and that he shouldn't correct the other children like that. When Mom and Gary finished talking, he went back into the playroom and told the other children that they couldn't play with that game anymore. He said it was his game and he didn't want them using it. Gary changed his behavior, but he still had a heart problem that showed itself in his controlling and selfish attitude.

After hearing this new approach, Mom again called Gary out of the playroom and sent him to his room on a mission to change his heart. Although it took most of the morning, Gary ended up changing his attitude before he went back to enjoy time with his friends.

If you discipline your child to change behavior but a bad attitude remains, then the discipline is incomplete. If you want honor, you must continue to correct until the attitude is changed. A child who adjusts behavior but continues to harbor a poor attitude needs to learn honor. If not addressed, bad attitudes just get worse.

Step back and ask yourself, "Why is this child struggling with a bad attitude?" This will help you focus your discipline. One mom recognized that her five-year-old son needed more sleep. "I was amazed at how much better our day went after I began enforcing an earlier bedtime." Another mom realized her nine-year-old needed to learn perseverance, the ability to hang in there when things get tough.

One dad reported that his daughter Jodi, age nine, often engaged in negative self-talk: "I'm no good," "I can't do anything right," "Nobody likes me." In this case, his daughter's anger was focused on herself, resulting in a bad attitude. He helped Jodi by making a list of the negative statements he heard. Later, after Jodi settled down, he showed the list to his daughter. "Do you believe these things?"

"Sometimes."

"Well, they're not true, but I think you say them because you're angry. It's not honoring to yourself. If I hear you saying these things, I'm going to have you take a break, and then we're going to talk about it."

With careful attention, all of these parents were able to help their children overcome a bad attitude. It took work, but the results were well worth it. Don't ignore a bad attitude. It directly reflects a problem of dishonor in a child's life. By disciplining for attitude problems and teaching your children a better way, you're helping them to develop a lifestyle of honor.

Honor Lesson #4: Create Honor Lessons in Life

Several techniques will help teach children to value others. A mother of two preschoolers said, "I teach my children that one way to honor me is to listen with both eyes. They think that's funny, but it helps them understand that we show honor by looking at people when they speak." Another mom encouraged her children to notice the delight on people's faces when they opened Christmas presents. She then used that fun observation to talk about giving small gifts of cooperation, appreciation, and encouragement during the day and watching the delight on people's faces.

Your own response to honor is important. When your son folds the towels as you asked and then does more by putting them away, your delight is his reward. Honor is a gift—that extra, unexpected act of kindness. Let your children know you noticed. Let them hear you bragging about how they did more than what was expected. Take time to tell your children when you feel honored, that you're pleased with what they're doing and how they're responding.

Too often, parents focus on what a child doesn't do, and they neglect to praise the child for the good things he or she did. This results in discouragement, and children may give up on honor because they think it doesn't work. Sometimes parents avoid showing approval because the child is expected to honor. One mom said, "They shouldn't expect to get rewarded for something they're supposed to do." This attitude stifles a child's desire to give honor. Be sure to point out honoring speech and actions when you see them in your children.

The Turanskys and the Millers went on a memorable vacation in Kenya after a time of ministry there. All eleven of us traveled together in one van, without air conditioning, for ten hours from Nairobi to Mombasa. We knew the trip might test our sanity and that there would be plenty of opportunity for dishonoring words. As with most long trips in the car, it was a recipe for disaster. We decided to plan ahead, and it was for this trip that we created the "Whoops and Ahhh" game.

We told the children that we had identified five types of dishonoring speech: arguing, boasting, whining/complaining, talking too much, and being bossy. Anyone who heard dishonoring speech could say "Whoops!" and people would try to guess which type of dishonoring speech they heard. Then we would work together to offer honoring suggestions.

When David said, "They have both black and white rhinos in Africa," Tim countered by saying, "No, they only have black rhinos." Ben said, "Whoops!" We identified the "Whoops" problem as arguing and suggested that Tim give a more humble response, such as, "I thought there were only black rhinos in Africa."

At the same time, all of us were on the lookout for honoring speech that includes praise, gratefulness, compliments, and affirmation. Megan said, "Thanks, Dad, for taking us here." I said, "Ahhh," and everyone laughed. It was catching, and several others added honoring speech to get the "Ahhh" response.

To keep it fun, occasionally Scott and Ed, the two dads, would say something dishonoring on purpose, gaining a hearty "Whoops!" Scott said, "I'm the best driver in all of Kenya." The comment gained a corporate "Whoops!" for boasting. The group suggested that it might be best for Scott not to say anything, at least appearing to be humble. Ed said, "That's a dumb idea," to his son, David, and received a "Whoops!" for arguing.

After arriving at our destination, we had to declare the game over lest people become irritated by the intense analysis, but it turned out to be a valuable lesson for all. We discovered that people tend to speak in dishonoring ways without even realizing it.

In another example, one dad wanted to work on honor with

his seven-year-old daughter, Diane, who seemed self-centered, always talking and thinking about herself. In the evening, he asked Diane to identify examples of a friend or family member who was sad, glad, or mad that day. Then he asked the question, "How might you respond to that person in a helpful way?"

They continued this exercise every evening for two weeks. After a while it helped Diane to get outside of herself, look at the needs and feelings of others, and then respond with honor. She decided that when her brother is mad, it would be best to leave him alone or to just ask a helpful question. With her friend who is sad, she could offer to help and then listen empathetically. When Mom is glad, Diane could enter into that gladness by listening to the story behind her happiness and enjoying the situation too.

Honor Lesson #5:
Model it

Children learn about honor from their parents. One father said, "I've tried all kinds of techniques for teaching my son table manners. It doesn't work. He still eats just like me!" We're models whether we like it or not.

---

i wasn't just coaching baseball that day,
i was coaching my son about life.

Vulnerability and transparency are important. Let's face it, honor isn't always easy for parents either. Some would love to say a few unkind words about that police officer or the boss or the president. How you respond to the decisions of leaders or to the news teaches children how to respond to you. The way Mom and Dad treat each other, even in disagreements, is an example to children of how they should treat others.

I (Scott) coached my son Josh's Little League baseball team one year. During our season, Josh and I would talk about the different coaching styles we observed. Some coaches were quite mean, and many had a problem with anger that came out in subtle and not-so-subtle ways. We talked about how the players must feel and how unimportant winning and losing really were. I remember one particularly vicious game. We were playing a team whose coach was determined to win whatever the cost. He yelled at his players, yelled at the umpires, and yelled at me. We lost the game that day, but I was winning in the relationship with my son. What's more important? I wasn't just coaching baseball. That day, I was coaching my son about life.

Josh continued to play baseball and, in his last year, won the Cranstoun Award. That's an award given to one player in the town each year who demonstrates outstanding sportsmanship, encouragement, and team playing. Josh may not have been the best player on the best team, but his values were rewarded in the end. We all learned a valuable lesson about honor through that experience.

One way to model honor is to talk about predicaments you face. One dad explained at dinner how two people were fighting at the office in underhanded and sneaky ways. He was caught in the middle and wasn't sure what to do. How could he be honoring in that situation? The family discussed the ideas, and then Dad reported the progress over the next week. He refused to engage in gossip and wouldn't take sides. He tried to remain objective, giving each person advice and being honest. This dad was able to teach his children that honor isn't merely a childish task. It's a success principle that works in life.

One adult remembers, "My parents forced me to clean my room and make my bed. I remember I gave them a hard time. I can see now that something else was going on. The way my parents treated me was firm, but it also showed honor. I didn't realize it then, but I was learning some valuable lessons about relationships." When parents discipline with honor, they must remove selfishness from their own hearts in order to discipline effectively. This is a challenge, but the results reproduce themselves in their children.

Honor is a self-perpetuating attitude in a home. When you model honor, your children will begin to mirror your attitude.

Honor Lesson #6: Appeal to Conscience

Although children may appear tough at times, their delicate consciences can be a significant tool for helping them to learn honor.

One day when I (Scott) was in the third grade, the PE teacher came into our classroom to adjust the student desks. He told the whole class to be quiet. Some kids were talking in my corner of the room, but it wasn't me. Nevertheless, the PE teacher came up behind me and thumped me on the head. It really hurt! I felt unjustly attacked, and I started to cry. I was angry with him and embarrassed that I was crying. I had done nothing wrong. I was so upset that I went home at the end of the day and told my dad. I thought he might storm in there and yell at the principal or the teacher and get him fired—or maybe something worse.

But Dad didn't do that. He taught me something about honor that day that has stayed with me for many years. He said, "Scott, I'm just guessing, but I'll bet that sometimes you *are* the one talking and goofing off and that you've created a reputation for yourself. Maybe that's why your teacher thought it was you."

With those words, Dad touched my conscience. I knew it was true. "I've got a suggestion for you," he continued. "I think you'll be surprised at the result. Why don't you go back to that teacher and tell him you're sorry for creating a bad reputation, even though you weren't the one talking yesterday."

That idea clicked with me. So the next day I walked into the PE teacher's office. Before he had a chance to say anything, I said, "I'm sorry for creating a reputation of being the one who goofs off. I wasn't the one talking yesterday when you thumped me on the head, but I realize that you thought it was me because of my reputation. I'm sorry."

The teacher, not knowing how to react, just said, "Okay." I turned around and left, feeling great. I knew in my conscience that I had done the right thing. The next day during PE, the whole class was doing push-ups when the teacher called out, "Turansky, come over here." I got up and walked over. "I just want to tell you, that was a pretty mature thing you said. That was the sign of a real man." I felt ten feet tall.

It's amazing what things touch a child's conscience. Sometimes it's a word spoken in sadness instead of anger. Other times it's a

Scripture verse graciously revealed by a parent. One mom told her son that he could be very successful in life but anger might hinder his potential. The boy was then motivated to work harder at managing his anger.

When disciplining his daughter, one dad said, "It makes me sad when you choose to hit your sister instead of talking things out. It also makes God sad when we don't choose to do the right thing."

Appealing to the conscience is different from using guilt to manipulate. It is not a matter of telling a child, "You're bad and you need to change." Instead, we are trying to convey that the child is a good person who has done the wrong thing.

teaching Honor to children is worth it

When you honor others, you often receive honor yourself. It can be self-perpetuating in a home. New habits develop, and the family actually takes on a more positive dimension. Jesus honored others by sacrificing himself. The apostle Paul says in Philippians 2:5-10 that Jesus humbled himself by taking the form of a man and becoming a servant. As a result, God exalted him and gave him a name that was above all names so that every knee would bow before him. Honor comes back to the person who knows how to give it.

The rewards of an honoring family are great. When parents and children honor each other, the family dynamic changes, and joy is the result.

I (Scott) came home one afternoon for lunch and Josh, age fourteen, had made me a special meal. This wasn't an ordinary lunch. It was fancy, with a cloth napkin and a nice place mat. The food came out in courses. It was a fun time for both of us. Josh was honoring me, and I was delighted. When children catch a vision for honor it will enrich their lives and the life of the whole family.

take it a step further

1. Using Ephesians 4:29-32, make two lists, one that contains characteristics of dishonor and one that describes honor.

2. Read Philippians 2:1-11. Name several ways that honor is demonstrated in these verses. What was the result in Christ's life?

3. Read Matthew 6:1-4. How can this idea be used in a family when demonstrating honor?

4. Look up the following verses: Romans 13:5; 1 Corinthians 4:4; and 1 Peter 3:15-16. What do these verses say about the conscience? How might you use these ideas with your children?

FIVE

A deeper Look

Mrs. Morgan felt discouraged. "I've tried everything, but nothing has changed. Just last night, Joel and Bradley were fighting again. I stopped them, got them to calm down, and then we talked about it. I told them I don't want our home to be a place of fighting. I want it to be a peaceful, secure place that's safe from the world. But it doesn't seem to sink in. They still wrestle around like wild animals. It's so frustrating."

Parents are hungry for answers and try all kinds of solutions. Some parents try to solve individual problems, thinking that by fixing the parts, they'll fix the whole. Others focus on the latest behavioral-change techniques that happen to be hitting the airwaves. These often prove to be quick-fix solutions, lacking the depth needed to bring about lasting results.

What parents need is a deeper solution that addresses how the family relates and works together and who they are as a family. Each family has unwritten rules that govern relationships. Because these rules of interaction are hidden, many families see problems but don't understand how to change them.

After years of working with families, we've discovered a fascinating dynamic that we believe is the key to helping families change.

the Network factor

The "Network Factor" is the combination of relating habits that dictate what's expected in family interaction.

How We relate

Every person develops habits of relating—including body language, tone of voice, attitude, whether they express their anger or internalize it, and so on. In a family, those habits become cues and triggers to others who react in predictable ways. Dad relates to his son Jack differently than Mom does. Jack, in turn, relates differently to Mom than he does Dad. This is where it starts to get interesting.

Dad and Jack develop habits of interaction that are both good and bad. For example, Jack may obey Dad but not Mom. Jack may discuss more personal things with Mom than with Dad. Jack may feel closer to Dad than to Mom but he knows that when he wants to ask permission for something he'd better go to Mom. Furthermore, Dad relates to Jack differently than he relates to Bill, his other son. Different patterns have developed.

The Network Factor reveals itself in a network of relationships and deals with relating habits. Mom gives an instruction, and her son argues. It seems that all Mom has to say is, "I want you to…" and her son automatically replies, "But Mom…." Parents may bicker with each other or make verbal jabs but don't do the same with the children. A teenager may experience conflict with Dad over and over again but get along fine with Mom. Two sisters may continually tease each other but relate well with their friends.

One father said, "In our family, conflict always leads to yelling. When someone senses there's a problem, the solution is to turn up the volume." Yelling is a relating pattern learned in family life. In another family, one mother said, "When we experience conflict, everyone gets quiet and goes off to their part of the house." This, again, is a pattern developed over time, an indication of the Network Factor's influence.

---

the Network factor provides predictability, and predictability provides security.

Why do these patterns develop? The Network Factor provides predictability, and predictability provides security. Even if patterns are dishonoring, they're used because they're known and comfortable. Over time, patterns become deeply rooted and difficult to change. Expressions such as "That's who we are" or "That's just the way we do things in this family" further cement these patterns. Family members are caught up in a web of behavior that seems impossible to change. They feel like they're in a dance, continually going over the same steps, stuck in the same patterns, and wishing the music would stop.

take a Look at your family

Take a moment to draw a diagram of the relationships in your family. Draw a small circle for each person who lives in your home.

These small circles should be arranged in a circle. If there are five people in your family, you'll have five circles. Now label each circle with the person's first name. If there is no dad, then you don't have that circle. If Grandma lives in your home, there's a circle for her. Take the first circle and draw lines to every other circle. Then take the next circle and draw lines to every circle so that all the circles are connected. Your diagram may look something like Figure 3.

Although we've only placed one line between each pair of

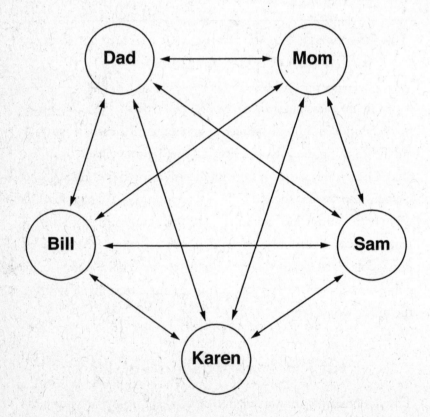

Figure 3. The network of relationships in a family of five

circles, ideally there would be two; the way that Bill relates to Mom is different from the way Mom relates to Bill.

Once you have drawn the lines between the circles, take another piece of paper and answer five questions about each relationship. These five questions can be remembered by the acronym PEACE:

- How are **problems** solved between these two?
- Which **emotions** are communicated or not communicated?
- How are **arguments** handled between this pair?
- What **conversation** topics are easy or difficult?
- What is the level of **enjoyment** in this relationship for each person?

If you've done your homework, then you should have several pages of observations about family life. You can identify the strained relationships, those that need urgent help, and those that seem to be holding together. Parents are often amazed at what they see. Patterns of relating jump off the page. The hidden rules of the family come to life from below the surface. One mom said, "I sensed something was wrong in our family, but this makes it all clear. Now I can see where the problem areas actually are."

Use the Network Factor to Bring About Change

Six-year-old Bobby has a problem with anger. Erratic outbursts disrupt family life and upset others. Bobby's parents are doing a number of things to help him manage his anger, but his mom and stepfather realize they need to address other issues in order for family harmony to develop. For example, Bobby and his older brother, Charlie, often use sarcasm and teasing to put each other down. Although it started in fun, it has become an unhealthy relating style between the two brothers. Constant put-downs and negative comments dominate their relationship. Bobby's anger is triggered, and these two brothers are becoming more distant from each other. Furthermore, Bobby's stepfather responds to Bobby's anger by withdrawing from him, relying on his wife to work out the relational problems. This puts distance between Bobby and his new parent and an unhealthy reliance on Mom to solve problems between Bobby and his stepfather.

Addressing individual problems is only part of the solution. Helping Bobby learn anger management will help, but there's more that can be done. Understanding the Network Factor's influence on family life provides added insight into healthy and unhealthy family interaction.

As this family identified patterns, they also looked for honoring solutions. Bobby grew in his anger management, and his stepfather learned new strategies for working directly with Bobby. Mom avoided getting caught between them, and the family grew toward greater unity.

In short, the family is more than just the sum of its parts. Dishonor in one or more members of the family can produce toxic effects on family dynamics. Other members of the family learn dishonoring ways of relating to the conflict. Acknowledging the Network Factor means that, when disciplining, you look for patterns to address.

One frustrated mom says, "After I disciplined Ryan over and

over for arguing, I would ask him what he was going to do right next time. Even though we discussed it, he wasn't able to do the right thing when he got back into the same situation. He just continued to argue. As my husband and I began to look at the Network Factor, we saw arguing as a pattern. We sat down with Ryan and explained to him the pattern that we saw. We then developed a plan to point out the arguing each time it happened and to ask Ryan to 'try again' with a more honoring response. Over time, Ryan was able to change his habit of arguing because we targeted it in all the different places we saw it."

Four-year-old Samantha runs her family. As a result, her parents have decided to sign up for counseling because they don't know what to do. As the parents evaluate the Network Factor, they see that Samantha uses whining and complaining to manipulate them to do what she wants. She refuses to obey and even threatens them when they won't give in. Mom often does give in because she desires a peaceful home and doesn't want a fight.

Defiance is a common Network Factor issue, creating a power struggle in family relationships. Once Mom and Dad see what's happening, they can develop a plan to change the patterns. They begin to overcome their fear of Samantha's defiance. Instead, they see it as an opportunity for their daughter to learn to relate in more honoring ways. They refuse to play the game according to Samantha's rules and, although she resists at first, Samantha learns a better way of relating to her parents.

One fascinating dimension of the Network Factor is that children respond differently in various environments. Tommy's mom is frustrated by her son's defiant behavior at home. Their relationship is a continual battle. Yet, she often receives positive reports from his teachers and his soccer coach. They characterize Tommy as respectful and cooperative. "Is this the same boy?" she wonders. Children may find it easier to be self-controlled, respectful, and obedient when they are with others because the network of relationships is different.

Here are four suggestions for using the Network Factor to infuse honor into your family.

Ask Different Questions

Does this example sound familiar? Caitlin yells from the hall, "Mom, Kyle didn't turn off the light in the bathroom!"

Kyle yells in his defense, "Caitlin was the last one in there!"

"Was not! You were!"

"Was not! You were!"

Unfortunately, parents sometimes try to figure out who is at fault or who really left the light on, fostering further competition between the siblings. Or sometimes Mom will come in and say, "Caitlin, you turn off the light." Kyle, of course, offers her a smile that says, "See? I gotcha!"

When a family focuses on honor, parents ask different questions. "I want you two to sit down and think about it. I'm not concerned about who created the problem. I want to see who's going to solve it. When one of you solves the problem, you may both get up." Instead of trying to play detective, Mom might say, "Who is going to be the mature one? Who's going to be a servant and turn off the light?" The children aren't being asked to work it out. Each is being asked to demonstrate humility. Parents who understand

and use the Network Factor ask questions that address honoring patterns. Who is going to be honoring? Who's going to be a problem solver instead of a fault finder?

Let's take another example: "Mary, I'd like you to go and clean up the toys in your room."

"But Mommmm!" Mary says yet again, rolling her eyes and huffing off to her room.

"Mary, come here, please. I can tell you're having a bad attitude by your tone of voice. If you can't obey with a good attitude, then I'm going to give you another job when you're done with this one. Now I'd like to hear a different response."

Using the Network Factor means you ask different questions. Parents aren't just trying to get a job done. They want to also address *how* the job is done. A bad attitude is not acceptable.

When parents ask different questions in a family, children learn to ask different questions too. What parents say in their interaction and discipline of their children determines what children are going to say to themselves. In this way, parents set the tone and atmosphere in family dynamics. Although they won't always express it in these terms, children will end up thinking, "My mom is looking for honor," or "My dad is concerned about my attitude."

Jesus wanted to help his disciples learn to think differently. He did it by asking different questions. To teach humility, he asked them, "What were you arguing about on the road?" (Mark 9:33-37). To teach Philip how to solve a problem using faith he asked, "Where shall we buy bread for these people to eat?" (John 6:5-13). The questions parents ask determine how their children will think about themselves and about their attitudes.

Change Yourself First

One interesting thing about family life is this: Parents need to change first before they can help their children to change. Your responses, attitudes, and actions contribute to their patterns of behavior—or at least your lack of response to a particular problem has allowed it to grow into a habit. If you want to help your child stop whining, you need to adjust how you respond to children who whine. If you want to stop your children from bickering, you must change how you relate to children who bicker.

---

parents need to change first before they can help their children change.

One day Marty, age eleven, came down for breakfast with his hair combed a little differently. That's all Jillian, age thirteen, needed to begin the day's battle. "Ooh, don't we look cute today," she said.

"Mind your own business!"

Marty and Jillian exchanged several more comments, ending with a duet of "Mommmm!"

This pushed Mom's button to step in with harshness, which was Dad's cue to leave the room. Meanwhile, Carla, age eight, sat quietly, afraid of the family dynamics. The Network Factor was at work.

Let's change the cues in this story. What would happen if Mom were to walk out of the room first? How might Dad solve the problem? What if Mom were to take Marty aside, discuss the Network

Factor between him and Jillian, then team up with him to change his responses to her dishonor? Each person has the opportunity to change the relating patterns. Furthermore, change in any one person results in change in others.

Consider the example of six-year-old Candice whining for a snack. Often whining is perpetuated in a family because Mom or Dad inadvertently encourages it. The whiner gets attention, even though that attention is usually negative. Many parents don't realize that some children don't understand the difference between negative and positive attention; they'll take the negative attention, and Mom is certainly angry enough to give it. While Mom scratches her head wondering why Candice would continue to whine when all she gets is an angry response, Candice seems satisfied that she got any attention at all.

Let's use the Network Factor to change the scenario. Now each time that Candice whines, Mom walks out of the room, saying, "I don't listen to whining." We aren't suggesting that walking out is the only solution to whining in a family, but do you see how it changes the Network Factor? The child no longer receives any attention. Then Candice will be ready to learn a more honoring way to ask for a snack.

One way to build honor in a family is for parents to apologize for an offense or admit a weakness. One dad said to his family, "I know I speak harshly to all of you, and I want to change." He then went to each of his children and asked, "How have I hurt you with my harshness?" It was a very touching discussion. Then the dad said, "I want to change, and I need your help. Would you please point out times when I'm being insensitive and hurtful to you?"

This step opened significant doors of communication and set a pattern in the family for others to also admit weaknesses and seek help from each other.

When you see a problem in family life, look for ways that you must change first before you can expect to see change in others. As you learn to respond differently, you will see an amazing thing: Your family will begin to change. It takes work, but it's worth it.

Use Triangles Wisely

Triangles develop when a third person is brought into a relationship. This usually occurs when two individuals experience conflict. For example:

- A child asks permission from Dad after getting a no answer from Mom.
- Dad criticizes Mom's discipline in front of the child.
- Mom steps in when Dad and daughter are arguing.
- Two bickering children appeal to Mom to solve their problem.
- A child tattles on her sister.
- A teen won't talk to Dad, so Mom becomes the go-between.

Triangles can be dangerous. When Zack complains to Mom that Dad's not being fair, a significant opportunity for both dishonor and honor occurs. When Christi goes to Dad with a proposal to get around Mom's instructions, Dad's response is very important.

In one family, Sue didn't go to her father when she had conflict with him. She told her problem to her mom, who told Dad. Dad then gave Mom a message for Sue. The relationship between Sue and her father required Mom's involvement in order to make it work. Mom thought she was helping, but solving problems in this way actually weakens the relationship. Mom's involvement is only going to push Dad and Sue further apart as they depend on her to keep the peace. Dad and Sue may find it easier to communicate through Mom so they stop trying to talk with one another. This is an unhelpful triangle.

If you're going to get "triangled in," enter as a counselor, not as a critic. "You're not happy with what Dad's doing? Let me give you some ideas of how to work with him." Or if Dad is getting triangled in, he can say, "Let me tell you what your mom is looking for." That kind of triangling is very helpful because you're teaching

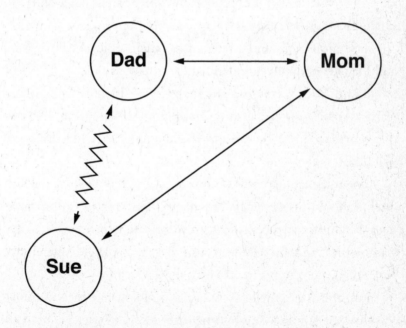

Figure 4. The involvement of a third person in conflict creates a triangle.

a child how to better handle the relationship. Your goal is to give suggestions and then send the child back to the first parent and allow the two of them to work it out. In responding this way, we teach our children how to work through struggles directly. This will strengthen their relationship with the other parent and also help equip the child for future relationships.

One common hurdle involves differences in the way each spouse wants to parent. Sometimes parents get frustrated with each other because they believe that they must not only agree on family rules but that they must also agree on parenting styles. Unfortunately, some parents can't accept each other's parenting styles. Parents must talk and be open to criticism, but sometimes we just need to accept the fact that the other parent has a different way of doing it. That can be okay. It's important for parents to discuss common goals and strategies for their children, but Mom and Dad are naturally going to handle situations differently. Dad's a dad and Mom's a mom, and they relate differently. Children learn valuable approaches from both kinds of parenting. Use the differences to make the most of the learning experience for your children.

One rule that helps this work is to say, "Whoever starts the discipline should finish it." If Dad starts, then Mom shouldn't take over or add her two cents, except in private with Dad. If Mom starts, then Dad should let her finish. Negative triangles often form when one parent wants to take over the discipline process.

Take the diagram you drew earlier, and now rate each relationship in your family. Put a number over each line identifying that relationship as 1-good, 2-somewhat strained, or 3-difficult. As you do this, you'll see which areas need the most work. Over time, patterns have developed, leaving distance in difficult relationships. Those individuals are stuck, often wishing things could be different but not knowing how to change.

Take time to think and pray about the relationships you marked with threes. Identify some things you can do to bring more honor into those relationships.

Because stress in relationships is quite intense at times and may appear unresolvable, some choose to diffuse it by bringing in another family member to form a three-person interaction. Sometimes this is intentional, while other times it seems to just happen as the emotion spills out onto others and they get sucked in. Unhealthy triangles quickly complicate family life, usually intensifying problems, as in this example: Mom is upset with her daughter and calls on her husband for help. Dad, instead of helping, withdraws, creating conflict between him and his wife. As the mother-daughter conflict escalates, Mom communicates her distress to her son, who proceeds to get into conflict with his sister for upsetting their mother. What began as a mother-daughter conflict has now erupted into several conflicts.

Every family deals with triangles. They represent opportunities for teaching honor and practicing it in family life. A wise parent sees triangles developing and not only handles them with honor but also teaches others in the family how to best handle those opportune moments. Triangles are common among children at the bus stop, in the cafeteria, or on the playground. Helping your children learn how to relate in these situations at home will give them an added edge in their relationships outside the home as well.

The Bible gives instructions in Matthew 18:15-17 about tri-angling someone into your conflict. The first solution is for two people to try to resolve the conflict between themselves alone. When that doesn't work, then a third person can offer assistance. This person may be someone from within the family, but an objective outsider may be needed. The goal of a triangle is resolution to the conflict, so it's essential that the third party be neutral, able

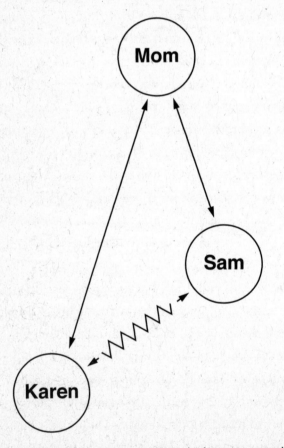

Figure 5. A good triangle is one that involves a third party as counselor.

to identify equally with both sides, with the goal of bringing the two closer and strengthening their relationship.

As you observe your family, look for opportunities to triangle into each relationship to teach honor, not to interfere. Perhaps you, as a parent, recognize that two of your children—we'll call them Sam and Karen—experience a lot of tension. Come in as a counselor or coach to help each child see things clearly and respond in more healthy ways. Use the opportunity to talk about honor, the importance of listening, understanding, forgiving, and communicating wisely.

Identify Nonverbal Communication

It's fascinating to watch families communicate. The signals and signs exchanged by individuals are often subtle but powerful. The message communicated is sometimes different than the words indicate. Tone of voice, facial expression, posture, and even silence often express a more honest and complete message. It's been said that only about 10 percent of a message comes from the words themselves. By contrast, 35 percent of the meaning comes from tone of voice, and 55 percent comes from nonverbal cues, such as gestures, posture, and facial expression. It's possible to stop verbal interaction but virtually impossible to stop communicating nonverbally.

Nonverbal messages communicate emotions, how we feel, and what we really think of something. A teen's long period of silence at the dinner table, for example, may increase tension and communicate as clearly as words that something is wrong. Unfortunately, nonverbal cues are often ambiguous and easily misunderstood. For this reason, it's important for parents to clarify the hidden messages.

A dad might say, "Because your arms are crossed like that, I'm getting the sense that you're upset about something. Is that right?" Simple observations of nonverbal cues can open the doors for clarification and discussion to take place.

Some nonverbal messages are quite clear. Squinting eyes or pursed lips may say that a child is unhappy with an instruction. These cues become hidden messages of dishonor. Don't let them go by unchecked. Children may think they're being honoring because they don't say mean words, but the nonverbal cues are just as hurtful. Verbal jabs, such as using name-calling or words like *stupid, shut up,* or *idiot,* would be caught and challenged in many families. Yet those same parents may allow sarcasm, angry looks, pouting, rolled eyes, or even manipulative silence to damage relationships. These nonverbal blows can hurt people just as much as careless words.

Stop for a moment and evaluate the nonverbal cues you use. When you give an instruction, is it done with a harsh tone of voice, furrowed brows, and a pointed finger? Or maybe sarcasm has become a way you correct a child. Some habits you've developed may be giving off unintentional messages of dishonor. Making adjustments in yourself will contribute to a more honoring atmosphere and also give you empathy for your children who need to change as well. Change isn't easy. It takes work, but the rewards are well worth the effort.

Many children and teenagers don't realize how often they communicate dishonor. Nonverbal cues may be under the surface and, although painful, aren't easily recognized. Use observations and questions to check that the message you're receiving is the one being sent.

If you come home from work and announce to your ten-year-old that you'd like to take him to the movies and your message is met with a wrinkled brow, how do you interpret that expression? Ask the question, "Does that look on your face mean that you don't want to go?" You may discover that your child is surprised by the opportunity to express herself verbally, not disappointed by it. Recognize that you are interpreting observed behavior, so check out your observation.

Children develop patterns of relating and sometimes incorporate a dishonoring posture or tone of voice unintentionally. It's helpful for parents to point out the message those signals are giving in order to provide children with realistic feedback. "When someone talks to you and you remain quiet, it gives the impression you're not interested in that person. He or she is likely to find a different friend to enjoy." Or "Your intense tone of voice leads me to believe that you're angry. I don't think you *are* right now, but your loud voice makes me feel like you're yelling at me."

Honor and dishonor are deeply embedded in the fabric of family communication. In the same way that a garden needs weeding to allow the flowers to grow and flourish, a family must weed out dishonoring communication. The task can feel overwhelming at times, but constant work will produce a beautiful flowerbed of honor that you will enjoy for years to come.

Use Parent-Child Evaluation Meetings

A parent-child evaluation meeting is an important tool for introducing new ideas and issues in family life. Once you've concluded that your son has a problem, develop a plan for presenting it to him. The parent-child evaluation meeting is an excellent tool for communicating new honor strategies in family life.

Several things make the parent-child evaluation meeting successful.

First, announce in advance that you (both parents, if possible) will have a meeting alone with your child. "John, Mom and I are going to have a meeting with you after dinner this evening."

The announcement heightens the anticipation for the meeting. One family with young children got dressed up for the meeting. These small things communicate that this meeting is important. Making an announcement in advance with teens and even giving a preview of the topic is an honoring thing for parents to do, since it allows teens to come to the meeting mentally prepared.

Second, meet with each child alone. Children have a way of hiding behind each other or diffusing the importance of the meeting when others are present.

Third, at the meeting share at least three things the child is doing well or that you've appreciated lately. Share positive character qualities you see developing. "I like how responsible you've been with the dog lately. You're doing a good job. I also like how diligently you've been doing your homework. It's been fun to watch you grow this year. I've also noticed your kindness with the baby, playing with her when she's fussy."

Then share one concern you have that will hinder your child's success if it is not addressed. Communicate it in a positive way. Give your child a vision for change by explaining the value of a more honoring response. Always give specific suggestions for appropriate behavior. Ask the child to work on changing, and agree to get back together within the next few days to talk again.

Sometimes making observations in this formal way is enough to motivate children to think about their actions and make changes. More often than not, however, you'll still need to gently point out the dishonoring behavior when you see it, in order to help your child recognize it too. In addition, you may need to set up a system of motivation. This could be explained in the first meeting, or you can wait until the second meeting, after it's clear that you need it. Use positive rewards for honoring behavior and consequences for dishonoring behavior. Meet regularly for a while to discuss progress.

> cHanging relationſhip patternſ tHrougH tHe
> Network factor iſ a valuable tool
> for infuſing Honor into your family.

---

it ONLy takeſ ONe

Changing relationship patterns through the Network Factor is a valuable tool for infusing honor into your family. If you don't like what you see in family life, examine the patterns and look for ways that you have fallen into a predictable rut with your children.

Many parents find this encouraging. One mom said, "At first I was frustrated by how much my children have to change. Then I saw all kinds of things I need to do differently. The Network Factor helps me to see how it all fits together. I realize now that I can be the person to initiate change in our family. As I make changes, my children will have to make changes too."

Scripture is full of Network Factor issues, teaching people new habits of relating. In the Beatitudes in Matthew 5:1-12, Jesus encouraged humility, gentleness, mercy, peacemaking, and other relational qualities. In Galatians 5:22-23, Paul explained the fruit of the Spirit, which includes positive ways of relating using self-control, patience, and gentleness. The Bible instructs people to love, honor, encourage, and serve others. These aren't just behaviors—they represent a lifestyle.

Jesus taught patterns of relating that make his followers distinct. In John 13:35, he said, "By this all men will know that you are my disciples, if you love one another." Christian families take godly patterns and apply them. This, in essence, produces a Network Factor of honor among family members.

Understanding the Network Factor will give you greater confidence that you can make changes in your family. Of course, the earlier you catch the patterns, the easier they are to change. And there's no getting around the fact that change requires work. But the energy you put into your family now will pay tremendous dividends later on. Young families can develop healthy patterns as their children begin to grow. Older families can learn that even deeply ingrained patterns can be changed. It's amazing how one family member can begin a chain reaction of change, resulting in a greater sense of honor. Maybe that one family member is you.

take it a step further

1. Read Colossians 4:6; 1 Thessalonians 5:15; and 1 Corinthians 13:7. These verses each contain the word *always,* which identifies patterns of behavior. What are the commands, and how do they relate to family life?

2. Read Romans 7:15-20 and James 4:1. According to these verses, why is change difficult? What do you think the solutions are?

3. Read Galatians 5:22-26. How does the presence of the Holy Spirit in believers affect family life?

4. A young brother and sister are arguing about a toy they both want to play with. How might you handle the situation, taking the Network Factor into account?

Honor-based parenting

A mother pushed her three-year-old daughter in the shopping cart at the grocery store. As they passed the cookie section, the little girl asked for cookies but Mom said no. The little girl immediately began to whine and fuss. The mother said quietly, "Now, Monica, we just have half of the aisles left to go; don't be upset. It won't be long."

Soon they came to the candy aisle, and the little girl began to shout for candy. When told she couldn't have any, she began to cry. The mother said, "There, there, Monica, don't cry—only two more aisles to go, and then we'll be checking out."

When they reached the cashier, the little girl immediately began to clamor for gum and burst into a terrible tantrum when she learned Mom wasn't going to buy any. The mother patiently said, "Monica, we'll be through in five minutes, and then you can go home and have a nice nap."

A man, having observed all of this, followed them out to the parking lot and stopped the woman to compliment her. "I couldn't help noticing how patient you were with your little daughter, Monica," he began.

"Monica? My daughter's name is Tammy. I'm Monica."

Parents often feel that way. If you could just talk yourself through the last few hours until bedtime you might make it to the next day. Parenting can be a real challenge. We learn a lot from our children, though, like how much patience we have—or don't have. With the continual barrage of decisions, conflicts, and problems, we feel as if we are wearing a number of hats but they don't all fit on the same head.

Parents wear the nurse's hat when children are hurt or sick. They wear the manager's hat to keep the schedules balanced and everyone on track. The cook's hat and the playmate's hat must always be available. They need the teacher's hat to home-school or to help children complete their homework. The counselor's hat and the coach's hat encourage children to work with others and to solve problems for themselves.

In the midst of all of this, the most important thing is not what hat you wear, but *how* you wear it. Parents often make the mistake of leaning to one of two extremes. Either they become a sergeant who dominates, or they indulge their child with too much freedom. Both of these extremes produce similar problems in children. Ask yourself whether your parenting tends to lean toward either of the following categories.

power-directed parenting

Rigid control and very little freedom characterize this approach to parenting. The home atmosphere is tense, military-like, and rigid. Parents may panic when they see their youngsters making their own decisions or pushing for their own ideas. They react with large doses of control and criticism. Power struggles escalate into bitter battles.

Martin's home was a difficult place to live. His parents were harsh and seemed angry with him all the time. "When I close my eyes, I still feel afraid as I picture my dad yelling at me or see my mom standing there with one hand on her hip, her finger pointed at me as she gives me that evil eye. To this day, I avoid eye contact with my parents. Those eyes meant anger and disapproval."

Martin's parents believed they were doing the right thing. They wanted to teach their son responsibility, respect, and obedience, but they used fear and domination as the motivators. "We couldn't even talk for five minutes without getting into a fight," Martin remembers. "My parents used threats and yelling as the primary disciplinary tools in our family. They found fault with almost anything I did. As a result, our relationship was cold and I developed a lot of resentment.

"I could hardly wait to become a teenager. That's when the power started to even out a little. My parents couldn't control me anymore. I was bigger, out of the house more, and making my own decisions. I began to take drugs and eventually got into trouble with the law. My dad tried to be rough with me, but I fought back. I just wasn't intimidated by them anymore."

Martin's parents were probably right about a lot of things. They knew what choices would be best for their son. Unfortunately, they failed to show honor, leaving Martin feeling that his parents didn't value him.

freedom-oriented parenting

Few limits and a lot of freedom characterize this approach to parenting. Parents ignore misbehavior or inappropriate actions, especially in public, expecting that any problems the child has will eventually be outgrown. Parents appear to be conciliatory and pleasant but may actually feel angry, tense, and anxious as their children push their boundaries. Such parents often feel taken advantage of and think that their children are ungrateful.

Living in Jackie's home was easy, maybe too easy. "My parents let me do just about anything I wanted. They gave me a lot, but I was never satisfied. I'd get angry, and to appease me, they'd give me more. I can't believe how spoiled I was. If they didn't like something I was doing, they'd try to make me feel guilty. They used pleading, hoping, and bribes to get me to do what they wanted, but they never came out and said, 'You need to do it this way.'"

Jackie's parents believed that they had to please their daughter in order for her to love them and grow up healthy. As Jackie began making more and more selfish decisions, they just gave up, hoping everything would turn out okay.

"I could tell that sometimes they were angry with me, but they wouldn't admit it. When we did talk, they tried to negotiate and get me to compromise. In the end, I did what I wanted. They said they wanted me to be happy, but they didn't help me to make good decisions. Much of the time I felt as though my parents just didn't care. We looked like a happy family, but it was fake.

"As a result, I learned how to run our family. My parents were inconsistent and timid, so I just decided what I wanted to do. I was often surprised by my parents' weakness and the things they did for me. I could basically do anything, and my parents would go along with it. As a teenager, I found it easy to experiment with all kinds of things. When I got involved sexually with guys, my parents pleaded but they never did anything to stop me. I ended up getting pregnant."

Jackie's parents had high hopes for their daughter and wanted the best for her. They knew that being a parent meant sacrifice, and they determined early on to give whatever was necessary. Unfortunately, they didn't realize that Jackie felt dishonored because no one cared enough to set limits or confront her.

different Approaches, similar problems

Not surprisingly, power-directed and freedom-oriented parenting often reflect the parent's own personality. Strong leaders gravitate toward the first approach. Those who easily sacrifice themselves for others may lean toward the second. These two styles form a continuum. Parents who spend a lot of time at one end tend to occasionally jump to the other extreme in an attempt to maintain some kind of balance.

Despite being at opposite ends of the continuum, these two styles have several things in common. In both approaches, parents fear conflict and use different techniques to skirt it, one control and the other avoidance. Also, in both cases, children grow up without self-discipline. Martin grew up in a power-directed family where children were controlled from the outside. He didn't have the opportunity to develop his own sense of self-control. Jackie grew up in a freedom-oriented home where self-control wasn't encouraged. Both learned to be sneaky and manipulative. Martin tried to get his own way without his dominating parents knowing. Jackie twisted her parents' arms to gain permission. Both grew up feeling insecure. Martin feared parental judgment, and Jackie wondered where the limits actually were. Children don't learn good social skills from either parenting approach, so they often become shy, obnoxious, or self-centered.

Parents don't usually decide to be power-directed or freedom-oriented, but over time their parenting style emerges. Some parents try to imitate their own parents while others react to how they were raised and try to do the opposite.

HoNor-bafed pareNting

Honor-based parenting is characterized by freedom within firm boundaries. The boundaries are large enough to give children the opportunity to explore, experiment, and grow, but firm enough so they learn definite limits for their actions. Honor-based parenting considers a child's wishes and desires as family decisions are made, but it balances them with the parent's wisdom and concerns.

Esther grew up in an honor-based home. "My parents were firm, but they were also kind. I knew they were looking out for my future, wanting to make present decisions in light of what might be best for me later on. When I looked into my mom's eyes, I saw warmth and gentleness. I really liked it when my dad gave me a hug or put his hand on my shoulder. We had a special relationship, and I'll always feel close to him."

Esther's parents believed that both parents and children should take responsibility for their own actions. They knew that sometimes parents had to make tough decisions and set limits. "When we had a problem, I knew I might not like the final decision, but I also knew my parents were trying to be fair, not just looking for the easy way out.

"When I was a teenager, my parents and I disagreed, but we talked it out. We would get angry with each other, but meanness and fighting were not acceptable. Sometimes we just had to agree to disagree.

"When I was fifteen, I wanted to go to a party with some of my friends from church. When my parents found out that no adults would be there, they said no. At first I was angry and felt they didn't trust me, but we continued to talk and they listened to me. In the end they still said no, but the way they handled it made it easier to accept. I look back on my teen years as a special time when my mom and dad were like coaches for me, helping me to develop the skills I needed for adulthood. I'm very grateful for the way they treated me."

Esther's parents knew how to balance limit setting and freedom so that decision making became a demonstration of honor. Conflict always contains temptations for dishonor, so they worked to control emotions, to keep communication open and honest, and to make empathy and understanding more important than winning arguments. The result is a daughter who is successful in relationships and adept at handling life's challenges.

Honor-based families aren't perfect, but they have discovered a secret ingredient.

"That sounds great, but you don't know my family" is a common response from frustrated parents. It may seem elusive, just a hopeful dream, but it is possible. Honor-based families aren't perfect, but they have discovered a secret ingredient. Honor changes both children and parents so that family life is handled differently.

At the second session of one of our parenting classes, a mom came with discouragement on her face. "I was all excited last week after the first session. I was determined to help my family change, but I continually had to discipline myself this week. Every time I tried to correct my children, I saw my own harshness and anger and had to stop and settle down. I don't think I got anywhere."

"That's the best thing that could have happened for your family," we responded. "The time you spend making changes in yourself now will make your work that much more productive in the weeks to come."

jesus Would Have Made a great dad

One frustrated woman said, "Honor-based parenting is too hard! I don't think Jesus Christ himself could parent this way."

That's an interesting opinion. Although Jesus didn't have any children, he did have disciples. The words *disciple* and *discipline* come from the same root that means "to learn" or "to be a pupil." Jesus was a discipler, and we are too as we work to teach our children.

What techniques did Jesus use in his interaction with his disciples? How did he balance time and relationships, love and control, patience and confrontation, time alone and time with others? Sometimes Jesus rebuked; other times he taught through stories. He encouraged. He set limits. He gave instructions, telling people what to do. He gave choices and let others make decisions. He gave people room to learn and to grow. Jesus honored his disciples as he worked with them. He did so many things that parents do, the comparison is amazing. What better model can we have than Jesus for every area of our life—including parenting?

If you've earned the title "Mom" or "Dad," then you must have also received your badge reading "Official Problem Solver." Whether you wear it or not, your children know you own one, and they know exactly whom to go to when they find a problem. "Mom, I can't find my boot." "Dad, I'm hungry." "Mom, would you help me with my homework?" "Dad, the light bulb burned out." "Mom, I don't have any clean clothes to wear!"

Similarly, people brought problems to Jesus. Interestingly enough, he often handed the problem right back to them—or he involved them in the solution as it developed. Perhaps you remember the story of the time when Jesus was preaching before a crowd of five thousand. According to the Gospel of Matthew, the disciples brought him a problem: "It's late and people are getting hungry" (see Matthew 14:15).

Jesus didn't say to them, "Here, get out of the way and let me solve it." He didn't lecture them. Jesus worked with the disciples and allowed the experience to help them grow. He said to them, "You give them something to eat," and then he helped them look for solutions. All they found was one boy and his lunch. But a miracle happened. One boy's lunch ended up feeding five thousand hungry people, and it was the disciples who collected the baskets full of leftovers. What a learning experience that must have been!

We saw a picture once of a mom sitting with an encyclopedia in one hand, a bottle of glue in another, extra shoelaces hanging out of a pocket, a tray of crackers and milk on her lap, an extra shoe on the floor next to a toolbox, and an open first-aid kit at her feet. A small boy is standing in front of her. "Okay, son," the mom says, "I think I'm ready. Go ahead and tell me your problem."

---

daily problem solving provides tremendous opportunities to teach children honor in life.

Bringing problems to parents is important, and children should be encouraged to get help when they need it. Parents, however, can use those problems to demonstrate honor to their children and to teach them along the way. Daily problem solving provides tremendous opportunities to teach children honor in life.

Jesus honored his disciples in many ways. He allowed Peter to make the mistake of denying him three times. No lectures or rebukes were needed; just a look from the Master's eyes, and Peter was overcome with remorse (Luke 22:54-62). Jesus forgave his disciples when they made mistakes. He spent time with them answering their questions and challenged them with his responses. Jesus spent time with people even when he was busy. He cared for people's needs when others suggested he move on. Jesus patiently explained and patiently listened.

True, Jesus didn't have any children. But he's an excellent model for parents who want to develop honor in their parenting. Jesus was a great discipler. As we become more like Christ, we learn to parent in more honoring ways.

HoNor-baſed pareNtiNg requireſ ſkillſ

Honor-based parenting may sound good, but how do you put it into practice? One mom shook her head and said, "I wish I had the time for this kind of parenting, but I've got to get the kids dressed and out the door in the morning. I have to work, then there's shopping to do, and I have to help with homework and get dinner on the table. My children always seem to act up when we're on our way out the door. I don't know how to fit this into my busy day."

Honor-based parenting does take work. But the most important thing doesn't involve trying to squeeze extra time out of your day. The most important thing is to fine-tune the things you're already doing. Five practical skills can enrich your parenting and make it more honoring. They provide the foundation for honor-based parenting.

HoNor-baſed pareNtiNg ſkill #1: be firm without beiNg Harſh

Some parents believe that the only way to be firm is to be harsh. Firmness says that a boundary is secure and won't be crossed without a consequence. Harshness uses angry words to make children believe that parents mean what they say. Some parents have assumed that firmness and harshness must go together, and the thought of separating the two is like listening to a foreign language—it sounds nice but doesn't make any sense.

A teenage boy closed his bedroom door and dialed a friend on his phone. "Hey, Ann. Guess what? My dad says that because I haven't gotten a job and I'm lazy, he's cutting off my allowance. Of course, I've still got the phone, so—[click] Hello? Ann? Hello?"

Firm? Absolutely. Harsh? Not at all.

Two things will help you to remove harshness from your interaction with your children: Talk less and show less emotion. In an attempt to build relationships, some parents spend too much time dialoguing with their children about instructions. They try to defend their words, persuade their children to do what they're told, or logically explain the value of obeying. This is counterproductive. Furthermore, some parents add anger to the picture, complicating matters.

Talking less and showing less emotion may sound strange because communication and emotional transparency usually lead to closeness in a family. These are good things, but it's a matter of using them in the wrong place at the wrong time. These two ingredients confuse the instruction process and don't give children the clear boundaries they need.

One mom felt bad about her anger but didn't know how to change. "I don't like being harsh with my kids, but it's the only way to get anything done. I get so angry when I have to say the same thing over and over again. One of the kids will come in while I'm making dinner and he'll ask for some ice cream. 'No, you can't have ice cream,' I'll say. Then the next one comes in and asks the very same question. I say, 'Didn't you just hear what I said? The answer is no!' It's like they don't hear me unless I'm yelling. My family has trained me to be angry because they don't listen unless I'm scolding them. If they would just do what I say, then I wouldn't have to get angry."

Some parents paint themselves into a corner, developing habits and cues that children learn to recognize. Harshness becomes part of the Network Factor, and parents find it impossible to make changes. Retraining requires work and almost always means that parents must change before children will change.

Other parents have talked themselves into the idea that their harshness comes from their love and that a loss of intensity shows that they don't care. When they're firm but not harsh they feel like robots, giving instruction without feeling. In reality, harshness contributes to distance in relationships; these parents have simply trained their children to recognize harshness as the cue that they mean business.

Firm limits can be presented with gentle words. One method parents can use for gently confronting is the "observe and run" technique. This technique simply points out inappropriate behavior and links that behavior to a character quality the child needs to develop. The parent doesn't try to engage in dialogue; he or she just makes the observation and then moves on.

For example, when Mom hears Corey make a sarcastic remark to his younger brother, she may say as she goes about her business, "That was unkind." When she sees her daughter quickly eat the last three cookies before Corey comes up the steps, Mom may say, "That wasn't very loving." These observations don't require a response, but over time they create a recording in the child's head.

What tapes are still playing in your head? "Turn off the lights… Big boys don't cry… Coffee will stunt your growth… Two wrongs don't make a right." Some tapes are helpful and some are not. By making continual observations about kindness, honor, thoughtfulness, and other qualities, you will build an honor tape in your child's head that will last forever.

Ordering children around doesn't honor or respect the child. A commanding or demanding attitude fosters resentment in children. Parents who use these tactics might, in the end, get obedience, but they don't get honor. They don't get it because they aren't giving it.

One mom said, "Whenever I ease up and try to be nice, my son thinks I'm willing to negotiate. He starts arguing and trying to persuade me until I get angry again." This mom and son have developed habits of relating. Mom needs to learn how to firmly say no without anger: "Sorry, I understand you have other ideas about this situation, but I'm done talking about it for now. My answer is no."

Mornings can be a stressful time for families. A single mom told how she addressed this with her children, ages nine, ten, and eleven. "I didn't like what I was seeing in myself. I heard myself nagging and prodding them along, yelling, 'You're going to be late!' 'You better hurry and brush your hair!' 'Get your shoes on!' So I gathered the children together one evening to introduce a new plan.

"'You three are getting older,' I told them. 'Tomorrow begins a new system in which you're going to manage yourselves. I've been doing a lot of yelling in the morning, and I don't want to do that anymore. So here's the plan. I'm not going to wake you up in the morning. Here is a new alarm clock for each of you. Decide what time you want to get up, and set it to wake you.'

"'What's the catch?' they asked me.

"'We're going to have checkpoints each morning. At 7:15, you need to be down for breakfast, dressed and with your shoes on, and your bed made. By 7:50 you need to have completed your chores and combed your hair. Those are the checkpoints. To help you be motivated to meet these checkpoints, I have something positive and something negative. Let's start with the positive. First, if you meet your two checkpoints each morning for five mornings, then I will allow you to watch a video on the weekend. But if you miss one checkpoint on a morning, you'll have to go to bed a half-hour earlier that evening, since you must need more sleep in order to get up and get ready.'

"The following day I was in bed, and I heard alarms going off and feet shuffling. I wasn't quite ready to get up, and I began having second thoughts about my great plan. In the end though, it worked. My children were successful at getting ready, and I didn't have to nag or be harsh. Firmness worked, and I didn't have to yell anymore."

Children and parents can be friends, but don't let that desire weaken your ability to set limits. Even in the most honoring of families, confrontation and discipline are necessary. Some parents seem surprised at this, somehow expecting that children will just want to obey. It's as if we expect our child to say, "Thanks, Dad, for sending me to my room. I really appreciate the limits you set for me," or "I'm grateful, Mom, when you make me clean up my room and make my bed." It isn't going to happen. If we expect our children to always appreciate our discipline, we're going to be frustrated.

One mother of three teens said, "I used to feel bad when I had to say no because I thought they'd be mad at me. Now I've learned to make a decision and enforce it because it's the right thing to do.

They may get mad, but I have to do it because I'm their mom. After they settle down, they know I did it for their own good."

Firmness doesn't need to be cold and distant. Eye contact, gentle words, and extra time can add a personal touch to parenting that helps children feel valued. Putting your hand on your son's shoulder, calling your daughter close to give an instruction, addressing a child by name, and speaking softly are all ways to show children that they're important. Children are not possessions to order around with harshness; they are treasures to treat with honor.

HoNor-baſed pareNtiNg ſkiLL #2: expreſſ ſorroW iNſtead of ANger

Often parents have a poor repertoire of discipline techniques, so they do what comes naturally. They use anger as a consequence for offenses and as a motivation to get things done right. Anger becomes the punishment that children learn to fear, and it results in distant relationships.

In honor-based parenting, anger is not an appropriate consequence. Instead, we should learn to reflect sorrow. Peel away the anger, and you will probably discover that you feel genuinely sad that your child is acting out or choosing to disobey. You see that their misbehavior may have immediate negative consequences and may even lead to an unhappy and unsuccessful life. Reflecting sadness is much more beneficial to the child and to the relationship.

I (Joanne) remember one day when my son, David, was eight years old. He was playing in the neighborhood with a friend. Although David's boundaries had been clearly communicated, he violated them and went down to the brook near our home. I was disappointed. David had disobeyed. I took him aside and had a serious talk with him, reminding him that the boundaries were set for his safety. He listened and apologized, and I thought that was the end of it.

Later that day I was looking for him, and he was nowhere around. I walked down the street just in time to see him coming back over the bridge on his bike, his buddy still down by the water. David had again violated his boundary, this time in direct defiance. I was so sad, my heart ached.

I didn't say a word about the problem. I told David that he needed to come home with me, and we went quietly up the street. This gave me time to settle my heart down. When we got home, David spent some time in his room. Then, when David was ready to talk, we had a discussion about it.

We talked about what David had done wrong and why it was wrong. I addressed the issue of trust, how I wanted to be able to trust him, and what behaviors show that he's trustworthy. We talked about the privileges associated with being trustworthy, and the restrictions necessary when he's not. As David and I talked about this problem, I didn't want to lecture or preach at him. I wanted him to understand, and I wanted to appeal to his conscience. He could see that I was sad.

David began to cry. This wasn't the angry cry of a child being punished. It was the repentant cry of a child who was truly sorry he had chosen to do the wrong thing. David had gotten the message, and his heart was touched. I hugged him and held him in my lap for a few minutes. I told him that I forgave him. We prayed together. Then we made a plan for the next time he was tempted to go beyond his boundaries. David learned that day the importance of obeying the rules even when no one is looking. I used sorrow instead of anger to teach that lesson.

There's a big difference between reflecting sorrow and laying on a guilt trip. Some parents use underhanded and dishonest tactics to manipulate their children. This is wrong. The key is to reflect sorrow or disappointment for poor choices or wrong actions while still demonstrating love for the child. Words like "Shame on you" or "I'm disappointed in you" communicate disapproval of a person rather than the actions.

Furthermore, some parents stop taking responsibility for their own feelings, blaming a child for ruining their day or messing up their afternoon. These approaches reflect a simmering anger rather than a genuine sorrow. Avoid manipulation by guilt. Instead, be honest, reflecting genuine sorrow for a child's poor choices.

HoNor-baʃed pareNtiNg ʃkilL #3: uʃe probleM ʃolviNg aNd deciʃioN MakiNg

Families make decisions and solve problems every day. Parents make some decisions that their children must learn to accept. At other times, parents can involve children in the problem-solving and decision-making process, teaching them to consider the ramifications of their choices for themselves and for others.

The use of money provides opportunities for children to make decisions. Parents can teach children how to save, be generous, and plan for purchases. In one family, Kari, age twelve, and Joel, age thirteen, were each given ten dollars for baby-sitting. Kari saved her money, but Joel spent his right away. A few days later when the family was at a museum, Kari and Joel both wanted to buy something at the gift shop. Kari had money, but Joel said, "I wish I had saved my money so I could buy something here." It's better for children to learn their lessons with small amounts of money early, rather than wait and make a costly mistake later on. Joel's parents honored him by allowing him to make mistakes. They didn't say, "I told you so," but allowed him to learn from his own experience.

Developing good decision-making skills gives children the ability to define a problem, look at consequences of various alternatives, and then choose the best solution among the options. Cooperative decision making teaches children valuable skills of negotiation, compromise, communication, and identifying alternatives.

Problem solving offers similar opportunities. When children are three and four years old they continually ask Mom or Dad to get them a drink. One family developed a creative way for the children to solve that problem for themselves. "We put a small pitcher in the refrigerator and told Katie and Mary that they could use the dishwasher door as their table, get their plastic cup from the bottom drawer, pour themselves a drink, clean up any mess they made, put the cup in the sink, and put the pitcher back in the refrigerator.

"It was fun to watch out of the corner of my eye," Dad said, "as Katie began pouring and spilled some. She instantly looked at me to see what I would do. Sometimes I pretended that I didn't notice. Other times I'd say, 'Oops. It looks as if you spilled a little,' without offering any more direction. It was satisfying to watch her response. She would grab a washcloth to clean up her little mess and take care of the problem herself. The dishwasher door is nice because it's low enough for them to work on, and if they make a mess, you just shut the door, and it gets clean in the next wash." This dad honored his daughters by communicating confidence in them. By allowing them to solve the problem themselves, he was saying, "I know you can do it."

Another dad agreed to allow his sixteen-year-old son to paint his room. "I bought him the paint, gave him some pointers, and let him go. I told him that he could paint right over the outlets because they were old and we would just replace them. The next day, after the painting was done, I bought four new outlets and a light switch. As I went past Nate's room, I dropped the bag on his bed. A few hours later he came to me and said, 'Dad, would you like me to replace the outlets?' I said, 'Okay, let me know if you need any help.' He had watched me do electrical work, and I thought the experience would be good for him. A few moments later, Nate came back and said, 'Should I turn off the power to my room first?' I'm glad he asked. I assumed he would do that!"

Helping children solve problems for themselves communicates honor to them. It says, "I believe in you. You have what it takes." Sometimes children need to let Dad or Mom solve the problem. You don't want a three-year-old cutting an apple with a sharp knife. Children need help from their parents, but much of the day-to-day problem solving and decision making in family life can demonstrate cooperation and teamwork as parents and children work together.

Parents can help their children learn to solve problems by asking open-ended questions and allowing the child to offer solutions.

Too often parents are quick to solve a problem for the child and end the discussion. Instead, try a good leading question: "What seems to be the matter?" "What are you going to do about that?" "Why is this happening?" When children respond with, "I don't know," be careful about launching into a lecture. Lectures can hinder the process of discovery. A parent may see Grant withdraw from the other children and say, "Grant, it looks as though you're having a problem. Come tell me about it." The goal is to get children thinking for themselves, not just wallowing in the problem or bringing it to you.

Honor-based parenting skill #4: Enjoy children according to their needs and interests

You may think this will be the easiest skill to develop. After all, you've been enjoying your children for years. But many parents, after careful examination, discover that they're enjoying themselves and inviting their children to join in. Parents determine the conversation topics, the entertainment choices, or the travel destinations. We often make choices we think will please our children, but in reality, we're loving them in ways that we ourselves would like to be loved. Many children are willing to join in, and the family can still end up having a lot of fun together. But focusing on a child's interests and topics of conversation can be a good way to show honor.

One woman was frustrated that her husband wasn't more involved with the children. "I know all about dentist appointments, soccer games, romances, best friends, secret fears, favorite foods, hopes, and dreams. My husband, on the other hand, is vaguely aware of some short people living in our house." Getting to know our children is foundational for honoring them.

One day when my (Scott's) children were young, I told them that they could each have thirty minutes of my time during which I would play whatever they wanted. Melissa, at four years old, chose playing with dolls. I never realized how long a half-hour was! We must have explored everything that one doll could say to another. I also learned that dressing a doll is like trying to put an octopus in a string bag. You just get one part in, and something else falls off. I realized then that I often choose to enjoy my children according to my own needs and interests instead of theirs.

Do you know your children's favorite colors, foods, or friends? Occasionally it's helpful to focus on their delights and desires. This requires talking with your children regularly.

The dinner hour can be a good time to engage your children in conversations. In fact, you can tell a lot about parental honor during family mealtimes. It's been said that more meals are ruined at the table than at the stove. Parents who use that time to continually point out proper manners and good eating habits, or coax their children to eat, often ruin any positive social time that might be possible. Nagging may be as impolite as sloppy eating.

Take an interest in your children's activities and stories. Listen to their ideas and plans. Show that you value them by paying attention while they're talking. Use the things you've learned to surprise them with small gifts of love. The skill of enjoying children according to their needs and interests is a way of honoring them.

Honor-based parenting skill #5: envision a positive future for your children

When we honor our children by envisioning a positive future, we focus on the good that we see and we talk about the long-term benefits.

Children believe what we say about them. If a parent tells a child he'll never amount to anything, he's likely to incorporate that into his sense of self, and it will end up becoming true. We can take that same principle and teach our children to see the good in themselves. When we envision a positive future for them, we give our children a way of looking at themselves that's honoring. In a sense, we're teaching them to honor themselves. What we say, they become. The qualities we focus on end up being the ones they see in themselves and work to develop.

Even if your children are still young, you can teach them how to imagine themselves in later life.

I (Joanne) tell David that he's going to be a great friend and husband someday, because he's so observant and sensitive to details. He has taken that to heart. The idea is self-perpetuating. When we talk about a positive future, we're giving a reason and some context to the things we're teaching our children every day. It gives a bigger perspective.

Take time to think about each of your children. Ask yourself, "What are they good at? What are they doing well? How will that help them down the road?" Even if your children are still young, you can teach them how to imagine themselves in later life. My (Joanne's) dad did this for me. As far back as I can remember, my dad has been my biggest fan. He's always believed in me. He taught me that I was capable of doing anything I set my mind to. We can each give our children that same message as we focus on them as individuals and celebrate their strengths, talking about these strengths in light of their future.

Looking ahead to adulthood helps parents and children maintain perspective. It reminds us that discipline has a greater purpose, contributing to future success. Children can then better understand that their parents are concerned for their future; as a result they, too, will begin to value its importance.

Developing honor-based parenting skills requires work. Your parenting focus up until now may have been primarily on your children and the changes needed in them. Remember that the Network Factor often requires change in several people at the same time. Once you make changes, it will be easier for you to ask others to make changes as well.

take it a step further

1. Power-directed parenting can be oppressive in the home. What are some examples of ways parents dishonor their children with too much control?

2. Freedom-oriented parenting gives children more than what's good for them. Read Hebrews 12:10-11. Describe a character quality you learned as the result of firm discipline, either from a parent, boss, teacher, or other authority.

3. How can you develop firmness without harshness? If you're already doing it, what makes it work for you?

4. Read Mark 6:34-44. List several ways Jesus involved his disciples in this miracle. How can you follow Christ's example of turning problems into learning experiences?

5. List at least one positive quality you see in each of your children. How might that quality help them to be successful adults? Take time to tell them about it.

SEVEN

HONor oNe ANotHer— eveN Your brotHerſ aNd ſiſterſ!

Arnold, age eight, wrote: "Dear Pastor, I know God loves everybody, but he never met my sister. Yours sincerely, Arnold."

One of the greatest sources of frustration for parents is sibling conflict. Parents often feel overwhelmed by the continual teasing, put-downs, sarcasm, bickering, bossiness, tattling, temper flareups, meanness, and on and on.

Children seem to naturally compete with and compare themselves to each other. The task of helping children get along is daunting. One parent defined sibling conflict as "anytime my two children are in the same room at the same time." Another added, "Mine don't even have to be in the same room." Seeing the problem is easy; finding a solution seems impossible.

Some parents think that if they ignore the problem it will go away. One mom said, "When the bickering gets too bad, I just go in my room and shut the door!" In fact, many parents believe that the solution to arguing and bickering is to allow children to "fight it out." Other parents choose another alternative: When their children struggle, they separate them and try to keep them apart in order to maintain peace. They imitate a referee at a boxing match, breaking up the conflict and sending the fighters to their opposite corners. Unfortunately, continually separating children doesn't solve the problem either. In fact, the children often come back again to fight some more.

We believe that both of these solutions are inadequate because they lack the depth needed to bring about lasting change. When parents only separate the offenders or walk away, they miss valuable opportunities to help their children grow. Conflict with brothers and sisters is a child's first class in relationships. Your home is the classroom, you are the teacher, and honor is the curriculum. Each conflict situation becomes an opportunity for teaching children how to get along.

God created the family as a place to learn and grow. Within the family, children can learn to treat others with kindness and to respond in a healthy way to unfairness or perceived injustice. They can learn to tolerate irritations, manage their anger, and work closely with people who are different. Addressing sibling conflict isn't easy, but the work you do now will not only make family life more peaceful, it will help your children develop adult skills that will assist them for the rest of their lives.

The secret to family harmony is to teach your children to honor each other, but that's not easy. In fact, there are three roadblocks that hinder children from honoring each other: anger, selfishness, and foolishness. These roadblocks and their corresponding solutions provide the curriculum for "relationship school." Understand them and you will learn to focus your parenting on the right areas, keep your cool, and help your children improve their relationships with each other and with their peers.

Honor roadblock #1: Anger

Angry outbursts are common occurrences in most homes. Children easily become irritated with each other, often leading to hurtful words and actions. Little Bobby walks into his older sister's bedroom, and she yells, "Get out!" Two brothers race down the stairs, and one elbows the other to get an advantage. Soon they're pushing and shouting at each other. Little sister Meg starts to scream and hit when her older sister excludes her from a game. An important lesson in the relationship curriculum, then, is anger management.

Recognize Anger

The first task is to help children recognize anger before they blow up. For some, there seems to be little or no time between the trigger and the outburst. There are, however, in all of us early warning signs that anger is developing. Raised shoulders, clenched teeth, pursed lips, lowered eyebrows, and a heightened tone of voice are just a few possible cues. People are different, and everyone must recognize his or her own personal cues that warn of approaching anger. Sitting down with a child, brainstorming about early warning signs, and being transparent about *your* anger management can all contribute to a child's growing ability to recognize anger.

Stop Anger from Escalating

Once a person can see anger coming, the next step is to stop and settle down. If the irritation is just at a frustration level, such as when your view of the TV is blocked by someone, then a deep breath may be all you need. If the anger has become more intense, such as when the baby spills apple juice on some homework, the way to stop it may be to walk away for a few minutes. Sometimes children and adults become enraged, that is, they can no longer think rationally. The anger is controlling them. If this is true, they need a larger stop or break. The child or adult must get away, settle down, and then come back to discuss the situation.

When a dad sees signs of anger in his son, he may say, "Charlie, it looks as if you're getting angry. I'd like you to take a break, please." Of course, if Charlie blows up at his dad, that's just confirmation that anger is present and that a break is needed. With work, parents can learn to recognize the early warning signs of anger and teach their children to take breaks.

Anger is helpful for identifying problems but not for solving them.

After the child takes a break and settles down, a debriefing is essential. In a nonaccusing way, ask questions such as, "What did you do wrong?" "Why was that wrong?" and "What are you going to do differently next time?" Having a discussion around these questions will help children see the problem and know how to make appropriate changes.

Children need alternatives to their explosive outbursts. Healthy outlets for that energy include talking about the problem, getting help with something, or slowing down and persevering.

Anger itself is a flag. It tells us that something is wrong. Sometimes that something is inside the angry person. Anger may come from unrealistic expectations, for example. Other times, anger is caused by injustice, violated rights, or a blocked goal. Whatever the cause, anger is helpful for identifying problems but not for solving them. The person bent on solving problems with anger leaves a trail of hurt and pain. Angry outbursts create distance in relationships. Rather, people who are angry need to recognize the anger, stop and settle down, and then choose a more helpful response. Teaching children to recognize and manage their anger with siblings will help prepare them for life in an adult world.

Here are a few more guidelines for anger management in a home.

- Never argue with children who are angry. Have them take a break and continue the conversation later.
- Help children recognize anger in its various disguises: a bad attitude, grumbling, glaring, or a harsh tone of voice.
- When angry words or actions hurt others, individuals should admit their fault and seek forgiveness.

Becoming a Peacemaker

Children can learn to manage their anger, but that's not enough for harmony. Honor means that children do more than what's expected and treat people as special. In order for children to overcome the roadblock of anger, they need a vision for being a peacemaker, rather than a problem maker.

Peacemakers seek to bring people together in agreement and look for solutions where everyone wins. They think of the needs of others and try to make everyone feel better. A peacemaker honors others and promotes harmony, bringing joy into the family. That's why Jesus said, "Blessed are the peacemakers" (Matthew 5:9).

Philip is sixteen years old and has one brother and three sisters. "I used to have a problem with anger. Now I've learned how to be a peacemaker both in my family and with my friends. When I see some of the problems kids have at school, I'm glad my parents taught me early how to manage my anger. I look for helpful solutions when people are upset. The reward is usually a sense of peace in relationships, but there's always an internal peace that comes from pleasing God and knowing I've done the right thing."

Anger comes naturally, but it damages relationships and creates distance between family members. As you target this area of family dynamics, you will see your children grow in ways you never imagined possible.

Here are a number of practical ideas for helping children to become peacemakers. Teach them to

- look for common points, not areas of difference;
- try to agree, not disagree;
- work toward common solutions where everyone wins, not where one person wins and others lose;
- use love, not anger or meanness, as a motivation.

One single mom said, "The key for me was separating my four children and talking to each one alone. I was able to connect with them individually. Separately, we were able to look past problems to solutions. Since dishonor looked different for each one, I was able to talk about what honor might look like for them. 'You can be the solution here. Look for an idea that will please everyone.' Now, whenever I see one of them compromising or trying to please, I'm quick to encourage and praise. It's taken a lot of work, but my children are learning to be peacemakers, and I'm pleased with the results."

Tattling is one way that children point out problems rather than trying to make things better. It's important to teach children what offenses they should report to a parent and what they should try to resolve themselves or just ignore.

Sometimes a child should overlook an irritation and not be so easily provoked. If a child has tried to resolve the problem, and the offense isn't one to drop, then the child should report it to an adult. This isn't tattling. It's following a biblical model for conflict management. As we mentioned in chapter 5, Matthew 18:15-16 teaches that if a problem cannot be resolved between two people, then one of them should involve another person in the process.

Being a peacemaker means that children learn tolerance. Tolerance is technically defined as "the distance away from exactness that a measurement can be before it's rejected." Some scientists make calculations in very minute measurements in order to maintain the quality of an experiment. Their tolerance range is quite narrow. Exactness of time or quality of material is crucial as they work for highly accurate results.

People have an alarm in their heads that is set to a specific tolerance level. When they're irritated or annoyed, the alarm goes off. Each person's alarm is set differently. Just compare your answers and your children's answers to the following questions: How close can someone get to you before you start feeling irritated? How much talking can you listen to before feeling uncomfortable? How long can you put up with a repetitive noise before it becomes annoying? Children and adults have different tolerance levels.

The good news is that tolerance levels aren't permanently set. With a little work, children can change their tolerance levels and adjust how many times a day the alarm goes off in their relationships with each other. Honor helps children learn to value the person above the irritation.

It is fascinating to watch children when they catch a vision for being a peacemaker. The creative solutions they develop are encouraging. One mom shared this story.

> My eight-year-old daughter, Jenny, loves to be a peacemaker. She now sees anger as an opportunity to help. When others get angry, she takes it as a challenge, often starting with, "I've got an idea…"
>
> The other day we were in a store, and a customer in front of us in line was getting angry. Jenny looked up at him and said, "I've got an idea. Let's talk about something fun while we're waiting." At first I felt a little embarrassed, but the man responded and enjoyed a conversation with my daughter. I was proud of her. She was being a peacemaker.

Honor roadblock #2: selfishness

A second major cause of sibling conflict is selfishness, always wanting to be first or best. Children are usually self-centered and demonstrate this in various ways: boasting and envy (wanting the biggest piece, being first, or wanting the best seat are all examples of this). Children go to great lengths to prove they are better, loved more, or got there first. One dad found his two daughters counting the sprinkles on their cupcakes to see who got the most.

Envy

I (Scott) like to tell children the story of the guys in the Bible who wanted the best seat. In Mark 10, James and John asked Jesus if they could sit next to him. Does that sound familiar? When you have one child, there's a choice of laps to sit on. With two children and two parents, each child gets a lap. With three children, someone gets left out. In fact, when you're reading a book together, someone gets the not-so-good seat and they can't see the pictures as well. It's not hard for children to identify with James and John.

Why do you think the other disciples were angry? Maybe it's because they wanted the best seat too, but they weren't gutsy enough to say it. Jesus responded to them with a foundational principle, the same principle that children need to learn to counteract their own desire to be first or best. Jesus said, "If you want to be great in my kingdom, learn to be the servant of all" (Mark 10:43).

A mother was preparing pancakes for her sons, Zachary, age five, and Tyler, age three. The boys began to argue over who would get the first pancake. The mother realized that this was an opportunity to teach servanthood to her children. "If Jesus were sitting here, he would say, 'Let my brother have the first pancake. I can wait.'"

Zachary turned to his younger brother and said, "Tyler, you be Jesus."

Being a servant helps children grow out of selfishness. You can begin to teach this by rewarding the child who demonstrates a servant attitude. Children who give in may not get the first pancake, but they get a parent's praise, a much more valuable reward.

Life has a way of showing honor to the person who is a servant. My (Scott's) son, Josh, had jobs in various places when he was a teenager. He worked at the local Christian bookstore and at a flower shop during holidays. In each case they loved him and wanted him back. Why? Because Josh knew the value of being a servant—grabbing the broom, looking for things that needed to be done, and contributing to a positive atmosphere. Josh had a servant attitude and was honored because of it.

Children often think that if you want to be great or honored, then you need to build yourself up. Children naturally want to grab the best for themselves. In contrast, parents should honor the child who gives the other person the biggest piece or who lets someone else sit in the best seat or who can listen to someone else's story without saying he or she knows something better.

Being a servant doesn't come naturally. One way to help children develop a servant attitude is to teach them that fair doesn't mean equal. Every parent has heard the phrase, "That's not fair!" The basis for this statement is comparison. Children who rely on comparison to feel good about themselves often end up in conflict. They want to have what others have. They think they want to be treated the same as everyone else, but what they really want is to feel special.

Rather than trying to treat children as equals, it's better to treat each child as unique. Each of your children is very different, so why try to treat each the same? They have different gifts and needs. Treat your children according to their own uniqueness. Treating children as individuals and telling them up front that they will not be treated equally can help reduce some of the comparison in a family.

---

treat your children according
to their own uniqueness.

In one family, Robert had a problem with dawdling in the morning before school. He was often running late and needed frequent reminders to keep on schedule. Mom chose to set up a chart system to motivate Robert and included a reward at the end of the week. Robert's sister, Jane, complained, "That's not fair. He gets a treat, and I don't get anything." Mom wisely responded, "Robert is getting a treat because he's working on something in his life. If you'd like to work on something, I'll set up a chart for you, too." Mom didn't try to treat all her children equally. She knew that fair doesn't mean equal.

Boasting

Boasting is another demonstration of selfishness. "I know how to do that." "I can do that better than you." Children try to feel good by exalting themselves. They seem to say, "I can feel good about myself when I tell you how much better I am." Sometimes children think that because they did it faster or neater, they're more valuable. That's not the way God looks at them.

God's solution to feeling good about oneself is to please him. A servant attitude directly addresses the problem of boasting. A servant's reward is the statement, "Well done, good and faithful servant." Children must learn not to compete with others but to do the best job they can, comparing themselves only to themselves and the standards and goals appropriate for them.

Teaching Servanthood

Parents can help their children learn to be servants. Here are some concrete suggestions to help you out.

1. One way to help children become servants is to teach them how to listen. Listening isn't easy. Children interrupt, yell, and talk over other people, resulting in misunderstanding.

    One mom told how she taught her children to listen. "I use this technique whenever my boys are in conflict over a toy. I sit them down with the toy on the table and say, 'You can play with the toy as soon as you both agree on a plan. Remember, problems aren't solved by only talking; solutions come through listening.' I encourage them each to share an idea and listen to what the other is saying. I coach them along as necessary. I teach them about compromise, working together, and sharing, but I let them work it out. Sometimes they'll both be stubborn, and I'll have them stay there until they can agree on a plan. They must always report back to me before continuing, providing an opportunity for me to affirm unselfishness and cooperation."

It's fun to teach a five-year-old how to persuade a two-year-old or to help two eight-year-olds negotiate a solution. Conflict is turned into cooperation through listening.

2. Teaching children to affirm others before telling their own story is another important way for children to honor each other. Encourage children to say, "I agree," or "You're right," rather than, "I know!" Instead of launching into their own version of the story, "Well, I saw…" teach them to encourage the other person first. "That must have been exciting," or "You saw a fun thing." Good responses in conversations are, "Oh," "That's interesting," or to ask a question.

3. Here's another fun way to teach children to be servants. The "I Cut, You Pick Rule" helps children who both want the last piece of cake or who plan to split a candy bar. The technique actually comes from the Bible story of Abraham and Lot. They had too many herds and not enough grazing land, so they decided to divide the land between the two huge families. Abraham, being a wise servant of God, said, "I'll cut the land into two pieces and you pick which one you'd like" (see Genesis 13:5-9). This plan motivates the person cutting to be as equal as possible. In the story, Lot chose what appeared to be the better piece, but

Abraham was rewarded in the end, and, most importantly, their relationship was preserved.

4. Playing games is a good way to teach children how to be servants. Choose noncompetitive games and activities that require teamwork. Encourage children to work together to solve a puzzle, build a project, or reach a goal. Teach children to coach each other along. I (Joanne) remember when my boys were first learning to read. I created a treasure hunt for them with clues printed in simple rhymes. They had fun working together to read and solve the clues. They worked as a team.

Learning to be a servant honors others
in the family and brings honor
back as well.

---

5. Some families have a "Servant for the Day." This child not only sets the table and takes out the trash but also gets to sit in the front seat of the car, bring the mail in, and help with dinner. Throughout the course of the day, Mom or Dad has an opportunity to talk about more subtle aspects of servanthood that involve how children talk, listen, and even think.

Teaching children to be servants will promote harmony in your family. Becoming a servant will help children deal with the continual desire to build themselves up while putting others down. Learning to be a servant honors others in the family and brings honor back as well.

Honor Roadblock #3: Foolishness

Foolishness is the third roadblock that causes sibling conflict and hinders harmony in a family. Foolishness is acting before thinking, laughing at others, or acting without considering the consequences.

The Old Testament book of Proverbs frequently describes the foolish person. In fact, I (Scott) like to read these verses to my children. Do these verses remind you of things at your house?

A fool finds pleasure in evil conduct, but a man of understanding delights in wisdom. (Proverbs 10:23)

A fool shows his annoyance at once, but a prudent man overlooks an insult. (Proverbs 12:16)

A wise man fears the LORD and shuns evil, but a fool is hotheaded and reckless. (Proverbs 14:16)

A quick-tempered man does foolish things, and a crafty man is hated. (Proverbs 14:17)

A fool finds no pleasure in understanding but delights in airing his own opinions. (Proverbs 18:2)

A fool's lips bring him strife, and his mouth invites a beating. (Proverbs 18:6)

A fool's mouth is his undoing, and his lips are a snare to his soul. (Proverbs 18:7)

He who answers before listening—that is his folly and his shame. (Proverbs 18:13)

It is to a man's honor to avoid strife, but every fool is quick to quarrel. (Proverbs 20:3)

A fool gives full vent to his anger, but a wise man keeps himself under control. (Proverbs 29:11)

Children can usually relate to the symptoms of the fool. In fact, a primary goal of childhood and the teen years is to overcome the roadblock of foolishness and learn wisdom. Proverbs says that the wise person shuns evil (14:16), prepares well (21:20), makes friends (11:30), controls his anger (29:11), and is responsible (10:5).

Children often act foolishly, not thinking of how their actions might hurt someone else. Alice, age four, her brother, Andy, age three, and Emily, ten months, were together in the living room. The baby-sitter was in the kitchen getting some milk and cookies when she heard the baby scream. She ran quickly and found Alice pinching Emily. "Alice, what are you doing?"

"We're playing ambulance, and Emily is the siren."

Children are like that. Sometimes we want to pick them up, look them in the eye, and say, "Why?!"

I Was Wrong

Foolish children don't take responsibility for their actions. "I was just playing," "He hit me first," and "She started it" are common excuses for hurtful behavior. Blaming is the opposite of taking responsibility. Blaming is a sign of foolishness.

Teaching children to take responsibility is the first step toward empowering them to change. One way to do this is to ask the child,

"What did you do wrong?" as part of the discipline process. Ask this in an encouraging and helpful way, with an emphasis on learning from mistakes. No matter what others have done, children are responsible for their own actions; the sooner they learn that, the better. Blaming others is never a wise response. Having children say what they did wrong teaches them to take responsibility for their actions.

---

teaching children to take responsibility is the first step toward empowering them to change.

Anticipate Consequences

Often children will act carelessly or thoughtlessly and end up irritating others. This is foolishness. Children need to learn to anticipate the results of their actions and control their impulses that hurt or irritate others.

One mom told of a typical problem in her family. "On a cold winter day my daughter, Colleen, stepped out the front door to get a book she'd left in the car. As soon as she walked out, her sister, Aimee, closed and locked the door so Colleen couldn't get back in. Aimee thought her prank was funny, but Colleen was cold and irritated.

"I heard what happened and later took Aimee aside. 'It looks like Colleen didn't appreciate your little joke.'

"'I was just playing around,' Aimee said.

"'I realize that, but you were having fun at Colleen's expense.

It's good to be funny but if you get enjoyment out of hurting other people, then something's wrong. I know you didn't mean to hurt Colleen, but if you'd think about the consequences of your actions you'd make wiser choices.'"

The Stop Rule

Teasing is a common area where foolishness turns into conflict. Although many teasing games start out in fun, one child usually wants to stop before the other, resulting in conflict. One solution is to implement a "Stop Rule" that allows any child to end a teasing game by saying, "Stop." Even a parent, when tickling or teasing, must also obey the Stop Rule, demonstrating to children the importance of their words.

If a child says, "Stop," but the teasing continues, the child needs to be able to appeal to a parent who will enforce the rules. Julie, age fifteen, decided she was done playing the game of tag with her brother. Gordon, age twelve, didn't know how to quit and kept pestering his sister. Julie told Gordon to stop, but he continued. Instead of becoming mean and ugly to her brother, she went to her father, and he enforced the Stop Rule.

Know When to Step In

Children can be downright mean to one another. In fact, unmonitored sibling conflict can turn into habits of meanness rather quickly. One mother of three young boys said that her third child's first word was "Ow!"

Sometimes meanness comes from anger over a perceived injustice. In one family, the two teenage boys continually picked on their little brother, Danny, who was eleven years old. They put shaving cream in his shoes, hid his baseball mitt in the trash can, and tied string around the legs of the bed and dresser so Danny would trip when he got up in the morning. Danny never responded to them, though, and seemed to ignore their mean jokes. The brothers started to feel guilty. One day they came to Danny. "We've decided not to play mean tricks on you anymore."

"So, you're not going to hide my baseball mitt?"

"No."

"And you're not going to put shaving cream in my shoes?"

"No."

"And you're not going to tie string to trip me?"

"No."

Danny smiled. "Okay. Then I'll stop spitting in your soup."

The problem of meanness challenges children as well as parents. Some advice suggests that parents get out of the way when children argue and let them work things out themselves. Although this can be helpful, there's a point at which parents must step in. Otherwise some children become resentful, and others develop habits of meanness.

A neighborhood baseball game illustrates a parent's role. Two teams were playing baseball without an umpire. It wasn't long before the children were yelling at each other and arguing about the game. Hurt feelings developed, and the game became a battleground. An older child happened by and offered to be an umpire. He called players out and safe, relieving the tension and allowing the children to enjoy the game. An umpire made the difference.

What the children needed in that ball game, and what families often need, is a workable system of justice. As much as possible, we want our children to solve problems on their own. But when that becomes difficult, children need a parent who will enforce fair play. A workable system of justice helps level the playing field.

uſe ſibliNg relatioNſhipſ to teach HoNor

Anger, selfishness, and foolishness are three roadblocks to family harmony and the cause of much conflict. Learn to target your parenting in these areas. View them as opportunities to develop honor. Teach children to be peacemakers and servants and to be wise.

Sibling rivalry and disharmony have been going on since the time of Adam and Eve's children. In the Old Testament, Abraham, Isaac, and Jacob each fathered families where sibling conflict caused the family to break up. For generation after generation, children have struggled in their relationships with each other. It takes work to be a parent, and the challenges in this area can be intense. But the time spent concentrating on this now will yield great rewards later. Your children will benefit tremendously. When you show them how to honor each other, you're giving them a valuable gift. After all, they'll be relating to people all their lives.

take it a step further

1. Anger got out of hand between siblings in Genesis 4:1-12 and Genesis 27:41-45. What might the parents have done to prevent the disasters that occurred?

2. Read Philippians 2:3-4 and Mark 9:33-37. How is servanthood described or illustrated in these verses? Besides the ideas mentioned in this chapter, what other creative ideas might help children understand servanthood?

3. Read Proverbs 10:23; 12:16; 14:1; 15:5; and 18:13. Each of these verses describes foolishness. Give at least one example for each verse of what foolishness might look like in family life. What might be a solution to each problem that demonstrates wisdom?

4. "Fair doesn't mean equal" is a principle that can help parents deal with the continual problem of comparison among siblings. How did Jesus teach this to Peter in John 21:20-22? How might you apply this in your family?

5. Proverbs 18:24 says, "There is a friend who sticks closer than a brother." Since sibling conflict is so common, why do you think Proverbs characterizes brothers as close?

EIGHT

Helping Teens through the "Tunnel Years"

One young man loved children and could hardly wait to have some of his own. He had lots of opinions about how they should be raised. Thinking he had something to say about parenting, he decided to write a book—even before he had any children of his own. The title would be *How to Raise Responsible, Successful Children*. After his first child turned two, reality began to dawn, but he still felt he could write a book. He chose to make it a little smaller and change its name to *A Few Ideas About Raising Children*. When his child was in elementary school, he turned the book into a booklet and called it *Raising Children Is One of the Toughest Jobs in the World*. By the time his child became a teenager, he decided to just make a flier to hand out that read, "Help!"

The teen years bring challenges to families, and problems seem to develop overnight. One dad reported it this way:

My daughter is now thirteen years old. She used to be obedient and responsible. I would give her instructions and I might get a bad attitude at times, but she would generally comply with my requests. Our relationship was okay and we could usually talk together.

Just a few months ago things began to change. She's stopped talking with me and has developed a secret world that she doesn't want me or her mom to know about. I'm not only getting resistance to instructions, but sometimes she even refuses to do the things I ask. At times she outright ignores me. Other times she says okay, but then she leaves the task undone. Our relationship is explosive, and it seems that anything I say starts an argument. I'm not sure what to do.

Parents find themselves getting frustrated and upset with their teenagers. Some even panic or feel hopeless about family life. But it doesn't have to be that way. The extra energy that comes from these emotions can be channeled into productive activity that benefits both teens and their parents.

it'ſ ALL iN their Headſ

As children enter their teen years, their development enters uncharted territory. Not only are their bodies changing and becoming mature, but their thinking patterns are also shifting. From the ages of eleven to fourteen, young people enter a new stage of cognitive development. They begin to adopt a value system they can call their own and gain a greater ability to reason, question, and evaluate their world. Adolescence is a time when young people begin to think for themselves and make their own decisions.

Recent studies of the adolescent brain have revealed some interesting findings. Although the brain is structurally developed by age two, continual use increases its efficiency. In fact, as the child grows, new areas of the brain become available for use. The wiring has always been there, but the lights come on over time.

As children enter their teen years, their development enters uncharted territory.

The portion of the brain that controls emotions (the limbic area) experiences new activity patterns during the early teen years. That's why teens may experience moodiness, emotional swings, and a heightened desire for excitement and adventure. Unfortunately, the part of the brain that controls reason and judgment (the prefrontal cortex) develops more slowly and is often not fully mature until the later teens and early twenties. This part controls inhibition and judgment and helps teens govern their emotions and make reasonable choices. It's because of this difference in developmental progress that teens will sometimes make foolish choices that may even be harmful, such as drinking, driving after drinking, trying drugs, or listening to dangerously loud music.

Brain development further motivates young people to evaluate the things they're asked to do, the values they've been taught, and the daily choices they make. Subconsciously, they're asking themselves, "What is my purpose in life?" "What kind of person do I want to be?" "How do I want others to perceive me?" Questioning itself isn't wrong. Rather, questioning can lead teens to think more deeply about issues, seek solid answers, and develop personal convictions. In the process, teens may react to rules and regulations and may reject the authority of teachers, parents, and other leaders. Moving from childhood to adulthood can often leave teens feeling confused and frustrated. They know that they want independence—and often wish they could figure out how to get it without continually disappointing their parents. Their physical bodies have experienced a growth spurt, but their maturity level is rushing to catch up.

ſtartLed aNd threateNed

One of the goals of parenting during these important years is to continue to help children embrace a value system that will enable them to become responsible, healthy adults. That may not be easy. All the work of the early years may seem like a waste when a child begins to make independent decisions. One parent said, "I can't believe he's doing this. It goes against everything I've taught him for the past fourteen years."

Parents often feel threatened by changes in adolescent thinking and behavior. In fact, it's hard not to feel threatened, knowing that a teen may attack or explode at the slightest irritation. Teen actions and questions are often perceived as forms of rebellion, and parents have a difficult time judging whether this is a phase to be ignored or the beginning of a problem requiring urgent action. Images of a child joining a radical group, running away from home, or forsaking family values can cause parents to either react harshly or just give up altogether.

One mom felt hurt but considered her daughter's meanness as normal. "Aren't children supposed to hate their parents in order to ease the upcoming separation?"

Another mom had given up. "You just have to get used to their disrespect. Hopefully, someday they'll appreciate you. For now, there's no chance."

Misunderstanding adolescent changes hinders closeness in a family. Independent thinking is healthy, but disrespect is not. Choosing one's own values is important, but that experience should not be an excuse for dishonor. Parents who don't realize the difference can overlook valuable teaching opportunities. Furthermore, teens may appear hard when in fact they're still very sensitive. Their understanding of themselves is much more fragile than their actions let on. When parents dish it out the same way their teens do, teens inevitably are hurt. Teens are at a prime time for life-altering experiences. An offhand comment may make a lasting impression. So be careful what you say and how you say it.

Wisdom is required to maneuver through the continual relational land mines. Unfortunately, the challenges often take parents by surprise. One Saturday morning when Josh was about twelve years old, I (Scott) reminded him to clean his room. Cleaning rooms on Saturdays has been a normal part of the Turansky routine for years, but on this particular day Josh decided to try out a new value that went something like this: "It's my room. The mess isn't hurting anyone but me. Therefore, you shouldn't get involved in my problem and tell me to clean my room, since it doesn't affect you."

That's a common idea, and maybe you've heard it before. The problem with that philosophy is that parents and children aren't just housemates, living together and tolerating each other's weaknesses. They have a job to do. Parents have the responsibility of passing on character and values to their children, and young people have the task of learning them. One of the character qualities important in the Turansky home is neatness, and one of the ways we teach it is by cleaning rooms each week.

That makes sense to me now. But at the time I was threatened by the challenge and appalled by Josh's statement. So I looked at him and said, "That's the same thing some adults say to justify wrong behavior, and society ends up paying for what those people do in secret!" Josh was stunned by my response and quietly walked away. I could tell he was hurt. I'd won in the argument department, but I'd lost in the relationship department. I'd also missed a good opportunity to help my son explore a new value. I came back to him later and apologized for my intensity and for robbing him of the opportunity to test out his idea. (He still had to clean his room though.)

Some parents come on too strong and find their children pulling back further than necessary. Other parents dislike conflict and let too much slide by, also missing opportunities to influence their teens.

Another father, Andrew, recounted a valuable and painful lesson he learned as a parent. "I remember the summer well. It will always be etched in my memory as a dark spot in my relationship with my son. I watched a TV talk show that advanced a popular idea. The group took out-of-control teenagers and stripped them of their honor in order to break their wills. They sent these kids to boot camps where drill sergeants yelled in their faces. I guess for some kids it works; some of the teenagers seemed changed. But at the same time, it doesn't seem right.

"Nevertheless, when my son was sixteen years old, I decided to set up my own boot camp. It was probably the darkest time in our relationship. I determined to make him comply, and I sure wasn't going to use honor to achieve it. I got him a difficult job doing landscaping, and he had to get up before dawn each day. A couple of times he tried to sleep in, and I made him pull weeds in the backyard in his pajamas. He even tried to sneak off to Grandma's house so he could sleep in one of her rooms during the day, but I found out about it.

"I rifled through his clothes and backpack for cigarettes and drug paraphernalia. If he protested, I informed him that he really didn't own anything because it all belonged to me. I told him that I bought him his stuff, he ate my food and lived in my house, and I'd go through his things any day because they really were my things, and so on and so on. At times I even got physically rough and verbally intimidating in order to make my point. No sense of honor existed between us. After a few weeks of this, he wrote me the following letter. I've kept it for years now:

Dad,

I'm writing this letter to tell you how I really feel about you. I hate you. You've been getting on my nerves, watching me all the time. It doesn't matter who I'm with. You won't even let me ride the bus anywhere besides back and forth from work to home.

Ever since I started working with the landscaping company, and you yelled at me those first few mornings for not being on time to work, I knew this summer was going to suck. We've done some fun things, but you've given me no freedom! I can never say all this, so I decided I'd write you this letter since this is the only way I can get through to you. It's too bad we all can't get along. I think you treat the dog better than me!

Jacob

"Jacob turns twenty-one in a couple of days. More recently we've talked about that summer. Neither of us thinks I handled that situation in the best way. I've since changed my tactics and have treated Jacob with as much honor as I can muster. I'm still firm with him at times, but at least he knows I value him like another human being. Our relationship improved dramatically from that point."

It's sad to see the mistakes parents make. Unfortunately, many of us don't discover them until it's too late, leaving lasting scars on relationships. It doesn't have to be that way. With understanding and a lot of work, we can continue to enjoy our children during the teen years. If parents are prepared for the changes, the teen years can be a time of deepening relationships, not distance and pain.

Honor, Value, and the "Tunnel Years"

Honor provides significant benefits to families during the teen years. Through the use of honor, parents can skillfully maneuver through this time to help young people accomplish the goals of adolescence and learn valuable skills for success. In addition, if teens catch a vision for honor, they can make this time in their lives more productive for themselves and easier for all.

One teen honestly asked, "What if I can't honor my parents because I don't find them valuable?" In many families today, this is a very real question. How can a son honor a father who's a drunk or who abandoned the family? How can a daughter honor a mom who is overly harsh or abusive? How can a brother honor a little sister who whines continually? How can a parent honor a teen who has disowned family values? These are not easy questions, and they often provide excuses for dishonor on the part of teens or parents. Teens may find it difficult at times to value even the best of parents, but this isn't just a teen problem. All of us, at times, find it difficult to see the value in others. But when others' worth or value is not easily apparent, we can learn to honor by faith. Each person has intrinsic value to God and is significant and worthwhile to him.

There's usually a time in a young person's life, though, when the value of parents becomes unrecognizable. These years can become a faith-building time for young people, if they understand what's happening and trust God.

It reminds me (Scott) of the time I took Josh and Melissa on a canoe trip. We decided to enter the stream by our home, realizing that the water had to run somewhere but not knowing exactly where. We surmised it would end up in the Delaware River, which meant an interesting trip through the heart of Trenton, New Jersey. Guessing that at some point the river might go under the city, I was prepared to call Carrie to pick us up by car if we got stuck somewhere. As we started the trip, the river's path was obvious. We could see ahead and enjoyed looking around every turn.

Then a huge cement tunnel appeared before us. I thought this signaled the end of our trip. I scrambled up the bank and crossed busy streets, trying to find where the river might come out. About a quarter-mile downstream, I again saw water and it looked very much like the river we had enjoyed for the past hour. Unfortunately the tunnel was dark, and we couldn't see for sure where it was going.

Being an adventuresome lot, the three of us decided to go for it. We would *not* suggest that anyone try this, however, as many things could have gone wrong. Once we entered the tunnel, we couldn't see anything. It was pitch black. We imagined rats and other things passing through the water all around us, and we wondered if we would indeed come out where I thought we would. We used our paddles to avoid the sides of the tunnel. Eventually we saw light and came out at the other end. In the midst of the tunnel, there were a number of uncertainties, many questions, and even fears. It was scary. But we came out the other side safely, and it was a fun experience.

The teen years can be like that dark tunnel. Honoring Mom and Dad during the "tunnel years" can be quite a challenge. For some budding teens, it just doesn't make sense. The wise young person, however, will seek to honor his parents by faith, recognizing, as many have before, that this is only a tunnel and tunnels have a way of playing tricks on our vision.

---

the teen years can be like that dark tunnel.

Honor is a step of faith and requires that a person live life in a way that acknowledges God's care and control. Honor is easy with some people, but it seems that each person has someone in their life who's a challenge to honor. When teens learn to honor by faith, new doors open up in relationships. Some people have the misconception that you must like someone in order to show honor. That's not true. Honor isn't about liking someone. It's about valuing a person you may not like. As teens get older, they'll find others who are difficult to honor. It may be a boss, a church leader, a parent, or even their own child. During these times, they must trust

God and honor by faith. Who knows? It could result in an unexpected gift of honor that God will use to bring change in another person's life.

The following suggestions for teaching teens honor are divided into two categories. Both are important. The first is proactive and the second is corrective. Many parents are continually correcting, and they benefit greatly from the more proactive suggestions. Others don't know how to correct without creating World War III and find the corrective suggestions helpful.

take Action to develop Honor

Proactive implies looking ahead and anticipating challenges. Don't wait for a problem to manifest itself, but instead take advantage of the peaceful or successful moments in family life. Many parents are so weary of the battle that they cherish any positive interludes as a time to rest up for the next confrontation. It's at this time, however, when you can do significant work in the area of honor. Proactive approaches are positive and more productive than corrective techniques for developing honor in the family. Here are a few suggestions.

The Teenage Challenge

Before each of our children (in both the Turansky and Miller families) turns thirteen years old, we enter into a six-month project we call the Teenage Challenge. Some families have incorporated the Teenage Challenge into later teen years as well.

To create a Teenage Challenge, identify eight to ten honoring character qualities that would help your young person gain the most from adolescence. One of the goals in this exercise is to give young people an excited anticipation of the teen years. Define each character quality in a way that's meaningful. Next choose a Bible verse to memorize and an activity that illustrates the quality in practical ways. Here are a few examples:

Character Quality: Servanthood

Working Definition: Seeking to overcome self-centeredness by focusing on what I can do to care for, bless, and make others successful.

Verse to Memorize: Philippians 2:4: "Each of you should look not only to your own interests, but also to the interests of others."

Activity: Plan and prepare a meal for the family. Write down your menu, and describe how people responded to the meal.

Character Quality: Humility

Working Definition: Learning to value the ideas, opinions, and advice of others. Being willing to admit sin and respond with grace. Learning to say "I'm sorry" and "Thank you."

Verse to Memorize: Titus 3:1-2: "Remind the people to be subject to rulers and authorities, to be obedient, to be ready to do whatever is good, to slander no one, to be peaceable and considerate, and to show true humility toward all."

Activity: Take a survey. Use the tape recorder to ask at least ten people to offer their opinions about what you should do to make the most of your teenage years. Write a few of your favorite answers down in your notebook.

Character Quality: Forgiveness/Anger Control

Working Definition: Recognizing the indications of anger and learning how to control impulses. Responding with cautious action and modeling grace and forgiveness with others.

Verse to Memorize: Ephesians 4:2: "Be completely humble and gentle; be patient, bearing with one another in love."

Activity: List five pet peeves (things that easily anger you) and plan five good responses you can give or do. Record these in your notebook.

Character Quality: Respect for Authority

Working Definition: Submitting to the God-given leadership of those in authority, beginning with parents, and realizing that a person's attitude outweighs the issue at hand.

Verse to Memorize: Colossians 3:23-24: "Whatever you do, work at it with all your heart, as working for the Lord, not for men, since you know that you will receive an inheritance from the Lord as a reward. It is the Lord Christ you are serving."

Activity: Write a letter to two of your authorities and express appreciation and willingness to learn from them. Keep a copy of the letters in your notebook.

Young people work on the activities and report to Dad and Mom at regular intervals during the months prior to their thirteenth birthday. Establish a reward at the outset and celebrate at the end. The Teenage Challenge helps give young people a positive attitude about the upcoming teen years and helps them to visualize ways in which honor will make them successful.

Show Honor to Teens

Wise parents learn how to treat their teens with honor and thus model honor for them. Look for ways to treat a teen as an adult or even as a friend. When teens feel as though they're being treated with honor, they're often more open and receptive to relationships with, and guidance from, parents. Asking for an opinion and then listening to the response—or allowing a teen to be a part of a decision—shows that you value their input. Asking questions about their interests and then listening to the explanation demonstrates an acceptance of young people, even though your preferences may be different.

Honor doesn't mean being wishy-washy or overly lenient. Honor can be demonstrated in the midst of firm boundaries and clear expectations. Listening to objections or compromising about differences can be a helpful demonstration of honor, but be careful about abandoning convictions for the sake of peace. If you've decided that your teen can't watch movies rated PG-13 without your approval, then don't back down. Even when teens go to a friend's house, they should honor their parents' convictions.

Expect Honor in Return

Honor's a two-way street. When a teen asks permission or makes a request, use that opportunity to make a comment about honor. Privilege and responsibility go together. The young person who is demonstrating responsibility and showing honor receives more privileges. It's a natural part of relationships.

You can't treat people poorly and then expect them to do something for you. In the same breath, a teen may make a disrespectful remark and then turn around and ask for some money. Teens may not see the inconsistency that seems so obvious to the parent. That's a good time to talk about honor and even require an apology for the unkind word before giving the money.

One teen asked his dad to drive him to the mall. Dad was quiet for a moment and then said, "I feel uncomfortable taking you to the mall. I'm still feeling bad from the harsh way you asked me to leave your room an hour ago." The son was quiet, realizing that an unkind word now would surely mean no ride. Dad continued, "Why don't you think about how you're treating me, and let's get back together and talk about it in a little while." The son went away, realized his father was right, and came back a few minutes later to apologize.

Talk About Honor

Because teens are evaluating life and are opinionated, engage them in value discussions that involve honor. Instead of continually making observations within the family, look for honor and dishonor being demonstrated elsewhere. Newspapers are full of ethical dilemmas. Athletes, politicians, and entertainment figures often give good illustrations of honoring and dishonoring actions.

Ask open-ended questions. Don't be afraid to enter into controversial dialogue. In one discussion we had with teens about honor, a thoughtful girl said, "It sounds like kissing-up to me."

As we continued the discussion, another teen commented, "Kissing-up to a teacher is something you pretend to do on the outside to get something in return. Honor, on the other hand, is when you actually like the teacher and you want to do something for him."

Another teen objected, "I don't think you have to like the person in order to show honor."

"It sure helps," said another, as we all laughed together.

As we listened to the teens and they listened to us, we all gained greater insight into the concept of honor. More importantly, though, the teens didn't feel as if we were preaching at them. They recognized that we were interested in their perspectives on the issue.

Expect the Teenage Parenting Shift

As children grow and mature, parents must make adjustments in the way they parent. Some of those changes are minor or subtle; others are more significant. For instance, when that tiny infant comes home from the hospital, the baby quickly becomes the focus of attention. The infant sets the schedule for feedings and for sleeping. Often both parents adjust their lives around one small baby. However, as that baby begins to grow and develop, the parents change too. No longer do they jump up for every cry. A major parenting shift takes place when infants become toddlers.

As children grow and mature, parents must make adjustments in the way they parent.

Another shift must take place when children become teenagers. Rigid parents who don't make the necessary adjustments will experience increased friction and frustration in family dynamics. Teens need more discussion about issues and concerns. Discipline involves more explaining and talking rather than just requiring compliance. A parent may say, "I'm not going to make you give your little brother one of the cookies you made for school, but I'd like to talk about it. I'd like to hear what you're thinking because it seems selfish to me."

Parents still have the final word and have to make difficult choices, but the way the decision is presented demonstrates value for the teen. Sometimes conversations will end in disagreement, leaving parents and teens with a dilemma. Even that can be good, as both parent and teen try to evaluate what's right for that situation.

Russ, age thirteen, exchanged a trading card with a neighbor, Christina. After the trade, Christina changed her mind and wanted to trade back. They had established in advance a rule of no tradebacks, leaving both children in a predicament. Instead of forcing Russ to return the card, his parents asked some questions to help him think about the bigger picture: What's the right thing to do? Why? Is it possible to be right and still do the wrong thing? Russ went back and resolved the problem by giving Christina an additional card to make the trade more acceptable to her. He went the extra mile, making his own choice to solve the problem with honor.

Even the best of parents, though, must make some changes in the way they parent as their children grow up. Teens are moving from a parent-child relationship to an adult-adult relationship. Unfortunately, some parents never make the shift. They continue to treat their teens as if they're still eight or nine years old. Honor helps parents recognize the changes and make the necessary adjustments.

One single mom of a twelve-year-old son reported dramatic changes after she began to adjust her parenting approach.

> We used to argue about everything. I would say no, and he would continue to push. He would badger and debate until I either gave in or became harsh. I felt he was manipulating me, so I tried harder to stick to my no answer with little or no dialogue. This created more tension and distance in our relationship.
>
> Now I'm trying to be more honoring. I share my reasons and listen to his ideas. We are able to discuss more and often come up with solutions where we're both satisfied. Life is so much more peaceful and joyful. Sometimes I still have to say no, but I'm able to do it without being harsh, angry, or demanding. Because he feels understood, he can accept the fact that we disagree and has a more gracious response. My son and I are much closer and happier now.

Although you may be able to "control" young children, the key word for teenagers is "influence." Five words describe different ways you can influence teens.

- Teach: Provide them with new information or help them to understand another facet of life.
- Encourage: Remind them of the benefits of moving in the right direction.
- Entreat: Earnestly ask them to act in a mature, responsible, and wise way.
- Admonish: Warn, caution, or advise them by anticipating possible negative consequences.
- Persuade: Use relationship, rewards, and consequences to motivate them to make wise choices.

As parents make the teenage-parenting shift, they learn the importance of validating their young person's thoughts and feelings before suggesting how a different response might be better. Parents take on a coaching relationship with their teen as the young person learns to maneuver and interact in an adult world. Teens learn how to communicate with honor and how to express themselves in a helpful way.

One mom was trying to treat her twelve-year-old differently. "I'm trying to shift my parenting with Penny. The changes are good, and I see how valuable and necessary they are. Unfortunately, sometimes she doesn't respond. I then panic and revert to ways that worked in the past. Penny then feels hurt, and I feel as if I failed."

It's dangerous to respond to rebellion by coming on stronger. The concept of the Network Factor teaches us that change isn't easy. Talk about the changes. Be patient and resist temptations to revert to less-helpful solutions.

Parents can enjoy their teens on a friendship level, exploring their interests and sharing thoughts and feelings together. Make encouraging comments about your young person's maturity and character development as your relationship begins to take on a new dimension.

correct with Honor

It's not enough to be right when correcting a child. Many parents believe harshness is justified because a child is wrong. Parents who are right, but not honoring, miss opportunities to teach. They damage relationships and raise children who feel justified treating others harshly.

Harshness is dishonoring. Instead set firm limits and talk about your convictions. "I'm going to have to say no to that activity because sometimes things happen there that I don't want you to be associated with." Explain the reasons and the values behind the rules. It's important to let teens know that they might not always agree with you and that there are times when they'll have to submit. The way you communicate the final decision can show honor. "I'm sorry we disagree on this. I'm going to have to ask you to do it my way this time, even though you don't like it. I wish we could come to some kind of compromise, but I don't see one this time." Hopefully, as time goes on, they'll learn to trust your opinion and convictions. But most importantly, they will know that they're appreciated and valued. Unity isn't always achieved through agreement. Sometimes it happens because one person graciously gives in to the other.

Express disappointment for poor choices, but focus your disappointment on the actions or behavior, not the person. In fact, this is a great opportunity to communicate a teen's potential, which is hindered by a poor choice. "I'm disappointed that you didn't follow through with what we agreed upon. That's not responsible, and if it continues, I think it will hinder your success as you get older."

Responsibility and Privilege Go Together

In Matthew 13:12, Jesus said, "Whoever has will be given more." He was teaching his disciples that those who are responsive to his message will receive more insight. The same principle is true in life—responsibility leads to privilege. Too often, parents give privileges to children who aren't responsible enough to handle them. Just because a child is fourteen doesn't mean she is mature enough to go to a friend's house without supervision. Don't give privileges based on age. Instead, use responsibility as a guide.

"Mom, how old do I have to be before I can start baby-sitting?"

"The answer doesn't have to do with age. It has to do with responsibility."

"So how will you know when I'm responsible enough?"

"I'll see signs at home. I can tell if you're responsible by how you take care of your room and what kind of choices you make when I'm not around."

Responsibility is demonstrated in children in many ways, and honor is at the heart of it. Cleaning up after a snack, being honest in a difficult situation, responding to correction without blaming an offense on others, and handling disappointment with a good attitude are all ways that children can demonstrate responsibility.

Keep Character in Mind

Take time to identify character weaknesses and respond accordingly. Relating the consequence to the specific weakness can be more productive than just "grounding" the child.

"I sense an ungrateful spirit in you, yet you seem to continually want me to sacrifice. I don't mind helping you, but I'm going to say no this time. I'll watch and see if your gratefulness increases for the things I'm already doing for you." This type of response teaches young people the value of gratefulness, instead of just considering their own goals and desires.

A teen who lacks thoughtfulness about household chores may need a contract in which parents agree to drive to an activity if the teen agrees to clean out the car. This again forces young people to give up being demanding and to start thinking of the needs of others. Sometimes teens want to come and go as they please but expect food on the table and their clothes cleaned. Honor teaches teens to give, not just expect to receive.

Elizabeth, raising her fifth teenager said, "Alan, age thirteen, was diagnosed with ADHD in kindergarten. He is often assertive in order to control situations. My husband and I have learned over the years that what we see as areas of weakness can turn into areas of strength later on. Alan is daring, not afraid to try something new. This last summer he went on a mission trip and was the youngest member of the team. He did well and was more bold than many of the others. They found his assertiveness an encouragement." Elizabeth will be successful with Alan because she sees his strengths among the frustrations and is helping him to see them as well.

Make observations for teens and give them feedback about their actions. "It looks as if you're easily influenced by your peers." "You seem to be having trouble managing money." "Those words are unkind." Habits are often ingrained, and continual observations move the teen slowly to a recognition of others and how to treat them with honor.

A demanding teen would benefit from understanding the difference between wishes, desires, and demands. When a child comes to the dinner table and sees spaghetti, he might think, "I wish there were meatballs, too." Or he may express a desire by saying, "I want meatballs in my spaghetti." A demanding child, however, would say, "I must have meatballs with my spaghetti, or I won't eat it," and then treat Mom in a mean way. Teens must learn to move demands back down to the level of desires or even wishes. This will help them avoid becoming explosive when they don't get their way.

Some of the discouraging behavior you see in your teen may stem from what will eventually become a wonderful strength. They need guidance to channel their energy and build honoring character. Talk about character, not just behavior. A teen, struggling with doing a sloppy job with chores, may need to understand that thoroughness is an important quality to develop. As parents focus their discipline on developing character, teens can see its relevance to their growing independence.

Gregory and his friends were playing with a BB gun when one of them accidentally shot a neighbor's window. They all ran home. The police knocked on Gregory's door in the evening and asked if he was involved in the incident. His dad said, "Oh no. He couldn't have been."

Gregory interrupted, "I was with my friends when it happened." Gregory was actually showing honor by telling his father the truth, even though he might get in trouble. Dad not only thanked him for telling the truth but also commended him for the strong character quality of honesty he saw in his son.

Correcting teens is an unpleasant part of parenting, but it is necessary if you want to teach your teens to be successful and responsible adults.

Conflict Resolution Skills That Encourage Honor

Conflict is part of any parent-teen relationship because conflict is a part of life. The only people who don't experience conflict live in a cemetery. Some parents and teens resort to underhanded communication techniques, such as sarcasm, dirty looks, or mean remarks. The way conflict is handled in a home is very important because it builds patterns that teens will take into other relationships and eventually into a family of their own. Don't be afraid of conflict. Use conflict times to learn valuable relating skills, and then model and teach those skills to your teen.

---

conflict is part of any parent-teen
relationship, because conflict
is a part of life.

Use your emotions as flags to point out the need to slow down, talk more, and solve problems. Three reminders will help you to gain the most from conflict situations.

Learn How to Start

The way you present an issue often determines the response. Sometimes it's best to address a problem immediately; at other times, waiting a few hours is more appropriate. Wisely choose a time, place, and approach with the goal of not just rebuking, but correcting and finding resolution. "Lisa, I'd like to talk about the way you treated me earlier. Is now a good time, or should we talk after dinner?"

Learn When to Stop

Once a dialogue has developed, know when to stop. Some parents feel as if they must win an argument or come to resolution by the end of the conversation, so they end up pushing too hard. Other parents end a simple correction with preaching, bringing up the past, or making exaggerated statements about the offense. In any case, it's important for parents to know when to take a break or simply stop the conversation. "I think we'd better stop here. Things are getting pretty tense. We need to continue this conversation, but let's take a break for now. Maybe we'll think of some other ideas in the meantime to help resolve this."

Learn How to Listen

Conflict represents opportunity. Teens watch how parents handle conflict and resolve differences. Listening and affirming a young person's thinking is an honoring step in conflict management. "I understand you'd discipline your sister differently. Your ideas make sense. At this point, I'm the one who has to make the decision, and

I'm going to emphasize something different. But I appreciate your ideas." Affirming or validating a teen's thinking or reasoning is helpful for their development.

As parents talk with their teens, they must learn to tolerate criticism. Many discussions you have will open the door for your teen to criticize you. Don't feel threatened or take these jabs personally. Use them to discuss issues and explain your decisions. If you can be transparent enough to use yourself as an example, your teens will learn much more about life.

Asking questions can launch a teen into a discussion and give you an opportunity to listen. "Do you feel as though we resolved the issue we discussed this morning, or did you have some further thoughts?" Genuine questions can open the doors for teens to clear off their emotional plate and feel freedom in their spirit. We all wish others would agree with us; if they can't, then understanding and listening are the next best things.

teens need honor even when they don't deserve it

The teen years can be quite a challenge for many families. In fact, it's during this time that many parents become discouraged and want to give up. One parent made the observation that "Isaac must have been twelve years old when Abraham was asked to sacrifice him on Mount Moriah."

"Why?" asked another parent.

"Because if he was a teenager, it wouldn't have been a sacrifice."

Ironically, it's during this stage of a child's development that a parent's wisdom is needed most, even though the teen may not seem to want it. You can teach ideas and values, but the way you interact communicates the most about honor.

A teacher took a high school student aside one day. "You have a lot of potential. You're smart, and you write very well. I'd like to mention something else I've noticed about you here at school. You seem to have an attitude problem. You criticize other people in order to build yourself up. You have the potential to be friends with many people, but you're making some poor decisions. I think you're robbing yourself of some of the best things in life by your selfishness."

The teen was surprised by his teacher's bluntness. "No one has ever had the guts to tell me those things to my face before." That young person marked that day as a pivotal point in his life. Many a teen will struggle for a few years and then grow in great appreciation of a parent who was faithful, patient, firm, and loving. The teen years can be a tremendous opportunity for modeling the finer skills of honor.

Working with teenagers can be a challenge for even the best parents. Despite your efforts, you may find your relationship with your teen strained. Take those times to develop your relationship with your heavenly Father. Pray for your teenager. God is the only one who changes hearts. The ultimate solution for poor character is repentance and submission to the Lordship of Jesus Christ. As parents, you must honor God and trust him no matter what. That's the best gift you could ever give to your teenagers.

take it a step further

1. What do you think the word *exasperate* means in Ephesians 6:4 and how does that apply to teen relationships, especially when they continually exasperate you?

2. What makes James 1:19 difficult for teens? How can you apply this verse in the tough times with your teenagers?

3. The self-concept of a teen is often fragile, even as their actions and attitude can be hard and obnoxious. How can parents discipline teens in ways that bring change while protecting their emerging identity?

4. How might you "draw the line" with a fourteen-year-old daughter who's heavily influenced by style, wanting to push further and further toward a countercultural appearance to fit in with her friends?

NINE

tHe More You give, tHe better it getf

Is it possible to honor your family too much? As with many things in life, too much of a good thing is not only bad—it can be harmful. Families who focus too much on themselves become self-centered. Pete realized this was happening to his family. "We put such a high priority on our children that we made the mistake of removing everything from our lives that didn't directly benefit them. Sports, music, clubs, and activities filled our schedules, consuming every minute of our time. Judy and I felt stressed because of the busyness, but we continued to press on, believing that we were doing the right thing. We then realized the problem we were creating in our children. They were becoming more selfish, and we were encouraging it." Inadvertently Pete and Judy taught their children self-indulgence and a me-first attitude.

The family can become an idol. It devours financial resources, along with time and energy that might be used in other ways. Pete and Judy realized that, while honor in the family is essential, they had a higher calling: to honor God above all else. Nothing should take the special place of honor in our lives that's reserved for God alone. Pete and Judy began to look for ways to show honor to others. They developed a plan to offer hospitality to singles in their church, involving them in family life.

Ponder the words of Jesus for a moment. When describing the importance of sacrificing to follow him, Jesus said, "Anyone who loves his father or mother more than me is not worthy of me; anyone who loves his son or daughter more than me is not worthy of me" (Matthew 10:37). God wants our love for him to be greater than our love for our earthly family. This may strike some as strange. After all, how many love stories have you seen on TV where the guy passionately tells the girl, "Honey, I just want you to know that you are number two in my life."

Then imagine the girl crooning back, "Oh, darling, that's the most wonderful thing you could ever say to me. You're number two in my life too!" Second-place loves don't make Hollywood blockbusters.

Don't get us wrong. Family *is* important. But it's not the ultimate priority—God is. Take time to teach your children that they're valuable, but also remind them that they're not the most important thing in your life. This will give your children a precious gift as you model the importance of loving God and caring for others.

Some parents enjoy their family so much they just want to capture it somehow and never let it go. They know their children won't be young long, and they've heard those testimonies of older people who say, "If I had it to do over again, I'd spend more time with my kids." We don't want that failure on our conscience, so we move to the other extreme. We all want to enjoy the good times, but some benefits in life are gained through giving, not through hoarding. Honor is one value that increases as you give it away.

the Need is great

You are probably aware by now that honor is a declining value in our society. In fact, in many cases it's a lost quality and people are suffering. One dad reported, "We got a call from the school counselor, who recommended that our daughter get therapy. That was a surprise to us, because our daughter was very honoring, was open with us, and seemed to be doing quite well. I asked what the problem was, and the counselor replied, 'I'm not sure. Your daughter must be hiding something. She's so respectful all the time. She's just not like the other kids. I think something must be wrong.' We shared that with our daughter, and we all laughed together. We know that we're different, but we don't need counseling. We're continually helping other families learn how to develop honor."

Nowhere is the pain of dishonor more common than in the family. Hurt people are the norm. Marriages break up, teens run away, and many families are "families" in name only, with individuals becoming territorial and distant from each other. Almost anywhere you go, you find families who are struggling. Many feel hopeless.

As honor begins to grow in your family, you'll not only see the problems in others, but you'll know exactly what they need. Even your children will look at others and see that your family has something special. It's rewarding when my (Scott) children see problems in others and say to me, "I know what they need, Dad. They need to take your parenting class." Or, "I'm glad you don't yell at us like that." Those simple rewards confirm for us that we're doing the right thing and that we have something to offer.

One of the most exciting benefits of sharing honor with others is that it reinforces what we are learning in our family and strengthens our desire to do and learn more. One teen who learned honor at home was known as "the counselor" among his friends at school. Sean simply passed on what he'd learned. He'd say things like, "That's sarcastic. It's really not the best way to communicate what you want. Just tell him honestly instead of giving little jabs." Sean realized that something good was going on in his family and was grateful for the things his dad and stepmom had taught him.

When you give honor, it comes back to you. The family that is a blessing to others is blessed itself. The Bible contains examples of families who reached out to others. In 2 Kings 4:8-37 a family opened its home to the prophet Elisha. Jesus often took refuge in the home of his friends Lazarus, Mary, and Martha to relax, eat, and minister. As is often the case, these families were later blessed because of their extension of honor to others.

When our families can take a stand for what's right, others benefit and so do we.

One family visited a rest home to sing and hand out homemade crafts. They wanted to honor the older people by talking with and listening to them. One elderly woman was openly bitter, saying all kinds of harsh things. The six-year-old girl, after listening to the barrage of complaints and insults, said to her mom, "I never want to be like that."

Mom replied, "Yes, I don't ever want to be that way either. That's why we're trying to teach you now how to handle problems without complaining." That evening provided a valuable lesson on honor.

The more you develop honor in your family, the more you will see the need for it. We live in a world of needy people, many of whom cry out for love and care. Their pleas often take the form of dishonor, causing some parents to ask an important question, "Should I protect my family from the pain and bad influences of the world, or should we be out there sharing what we've learned?" It's a good question. The answer is that we should do both. Sometimes outside influences undermine the lessons we're trying to teach our children. But when our families can take a stand for what's right, others benefit and so do we. Some well-meaning parents think that isolating their family will protect them. Although protection can be helpful for a period of time, it's also productive to have children see the contrast between their family and others that are struggling or falling apart.

tHe vaLue of geNerofity

There is no time when we are more like God than when we give to others. Generosity opens *our* hearts as well as the hearts of the people who receive from us. Giving doesn't mean just money. In fact, money is one of the easiest things to give. It's much more difficult to part with our time, attention, loyalty, or commitment to others.

Giving can be exciting. Planning the surprise, delivering it, and enjoying the person's response all add joy to family life. When a family works together to be generous, something happens in the

Network Factor. Family members feel a sense of teamwork. They discover family pride as a result of giving.

Giving is fun, but doing it in secret can make it even more exciting. Sometimes families will plan an anonymous gift. Hannah, age thirteen, reported that she overheard Mrs. Robertson talk about losing all her encyclopedias when her basement flooded. Knowing that the Robertsons didn't have a lot of money, Hannah's family decided to replace their encyclopedias. They went to several libraries, asking for a used set, and paid a small price for a set that was newer than the one the Robertsons had lost. Hannah's family then decided to give the set anonymously, which meant more planning and careful strategy. Seeing a need and meeting it through an anonymous gift became a meaningful experience for Hannah's family, and Hannah saw that her observation contributed to the decision.

How can you make your family a place where honor is given away? We've identified nine suggestions for giving honor to others.

Honor favor #1: Modeling

As your family spends time with others, people will see that you relate differently. You treat each other with honor, even under pressure.

Many families look good on the outside. They try to impress others and appear to be nice. It doesn't take much, though, to reveal their true character. A little extra pressure, conflict, or disagreement moves them to their normal patterns, separating those who are actually developing honor from those who are just putting on an act. If a family isn't practicing honor, then they don't have the skills to make it work. One husband tried to bring up a sensitive issue, and the wife looked out the corner of her eye, gave a big phony smile, and said, "Not now, dear." Everyone knew by the tone of her voice that she meant, "Don't make such silly suggestions." It was not an honoring reply.

The way you talk, disagree, correct, and interrupt each other demonstrate honor. If you regularly practice patience and gracious speech, others will see it when you relate in public and will want to know why or how. Many parents have told us that, after putting our teaching into practice, they go into a store and the clerk says, "My, your children are so well behaved." Some will think you have easy children. They won't know how much work it's taken to get this far!

Furthermore, your children become little missionaries of honor as they go into the homes of others. All they're doing is practicing the things they've learned in your family. One day, my (Joanne's) son Timothy was over at a friend's house. When I picked him up, the friend's mother was eager to tell me about the fun the boys had. "Timothy is welcome here anytime. He brings out the best in Kenny." When children learn honor at home, they naturally practice it with their friends as well.

Honor favor #2: Hospitality

Opening your home is an excellent way to extend grace and honor to others. We live in a compartmentalized society. Many of the entertainment options today decrease interaction between people and leave them feeling lonely. It's an honor to be invited over for dinner or for an evening of games and activities.

Carrie and I (Scott) met Ron and Tina Griffith, who had

twenty-one children, most of whom were adopted. We knew from experience that when family size increases, people stop inviting you over for dinner—and we only had seven in our family. We decided to invite the Griffiths over one Friday evening. Our children still talk about watching them arrive in their bus. They kept getting out, more and more of them. Josh said, "Look at that. They keep coming and coming and coming." We had a great time making more hamburgers and hot dogs than could fit on our grill and finishing up two gallons of ice cream for dessert. The Turansky family used hospitality to show honor to others that evening.

One week, when our son Ben was six years old, some tree cutters were working in our neighborhood. Ben talked to them every day and enjoyed watching them work. The workmen taught Ben all about trimming trees and enjoyed his curiosity and friendliness. Ben asked us if he could invite the workers over for breakfast the next morning and, surprisingly, they were interested in coming. We set up a nice breakfast of pancakes for them to enjoy out on the picnic table with just Ben. I encouraged Ben to pray for the food as they all arrived, which he did. That day, Ben enjoyed giving the gift of hospitality to his new friends.

HoNor favor #3: MiNistry

When families minister to others, they work as a team. Not only are people honored, but the family is blessed as each family member contributes. A sense of accomplishment accompanies the work, and honor is perpetuated in the home.

The Peterson family sings together and enjoys sharing their gift in churches and nursing homes. Each person's voice is important as they work together as a team. The family benefits from the camaraderie, and others are honored too.

Churches and Christian organizations need volunteers on a regular basis. Look for opportunities for your family to minister together and to share honor with others. My (Joanne's) husband, Ed, and son David worked together in the four-year-old Sunday school class at our church. The shared experience brought closeness to them and helped to meet a need.

Honor Favor #4: Service

Whereas ministry tends to have some spiritual dimension, service usually focuses on tasks that need to be done. One family volunteered for a "clean the park day." Doing yard work at the church or washing a car for the senior down the street are ways that families can reach out. They serve others to honor them, expecting nothing in return but the satisfaction of a job well done.

Sometimes children connect work with pay. They believe that if they work, they ought to receive some kind of compensation. Service is a way of showing children that sometimes we give of our time and energy without expecting anything in return. We just want to spread honor to others and bless them.

Honor Favor #5: Generosity

One of the reasons God gives financial resources or a lack of them is to connect people through giving. As you have financial resources available, consider how God might use your family to honor others. Have a family bank and choose a missionary or needy family to give the money to. Allow children to help make the decision and deliver the money, when possible. One family took some money, purchased baby supplies, and gave them to a single mom. Another family gave a special gift to the children of a missionary at Christmas. Yet another family tithed (gave 10 percent of) their Halloween candy and sent it to missionaries in Africa.

Honoring others requires that families plan to have a little extra. Many people spend all they make—plus more—leaving themselves restricted, with nothing to give. Reserve a little extra money, time, and energy, so you can share it with others.

Honor favor #6: prayer

Regularly pray for others. Take an extra few minutes before a family meal to list prayer requests. Report back as those prayers are answered. Encourage children to focus on others in their prayers. Many children thank God for the nice day and then focus on their own enjoyment and needs. Help children think beyond themselves by discussing needs and then interceding for them.

When friends or family members tell you about needs, share these needs with your children and take a few minutes to pray together. As you listen to a news broadcast or read the newspaper, think about the people behind the stories. Pray for Christians in other parts of the world. When disaster or violence strikes, pray for the missionaries who might be affected. Children may not be able to help in tangible ways, but they can pray. Honoring others through prayer will bring blessings to your family as well.

Honor favor #7: Speech

Demonstrating honor with our speech can be difficult. Words come out of our mouths before we know it. It's culturally acceptable to put others down, complain about leaders, and speak dishonorably about individuals. Families can be a good place to practice nurturing speech. How do you talk about a leader with whom you disagree? How do you tell a story that contains dishonoring information about a celebrity or sports figure? How do you speak about Grandma's weaknesses or an aunt or uncle who has some problems?

Sometimes it's best to be quiet and resist the temptation to tell that juicy story. Other times, it's best to give people the benefit of the doubt and speak graciously about them. In any case, reflect honor in the way you speak about others.

One father saw how his comments about people affected his family. "I realized that I had given my children an impression of my coworkers. At a company family picnic my son asked me, 'Dad, is that Ellen with the big mouth?' I realized that I needed to speak graciously about others because it affects how my children think and the impressions they have. I'm teaching my children how to think about the president or governor by the way I speak about them. I'm much more careful now about honoring people in my speech."

Honor favor #8: Helping others in conflict

The resources for handling conflict equip a person to have healthy relationships. Unfortunately, many people don't have the skills to address conflict. Once your family has learned to handle conflict in honoring ways, you can pass those skills on to others.

One mom told how her son, age ten, came home from playing at the park and said, "'I left because the boys were fighting. They can't decide how to divide up teams. You could help us, Mom. You know how to do it so everyone ends up feeling good.' We went back over to the park, and I asked the boys if they needed help. They allowed me to help them resolve the problem in an honoring way."

After hearing that Aaron and Cynthia were thinking about getting a divorce, the Davis family invited them to come and live in their home for a couple of weeks. Just living in an honoring home made an impression. The Davis family taught this couple how to communicate more effectively and learn to value each other. This gave them a new vision for their relationship.

Honor favor #9: Adopting others

Adoption is establishing a special, committed relationship over time. Sometimes that adoption is formal, as when Carrie and I (Scott) adopted Megan and Elizabeth into our family. We've learned a tremendous amount from our girls, and they've brought a lot of joy into our lives. But sometimes the adoption is less formal, as singles are adopted into a family or an older person becomes a substitute grandparent.

One family adopted Harriet, an eighty-two-year-old widow, to be their friend. Harriet joined the family on Thanksgiving and Christmas, bringing joy to all. The family brought Harriet cookies and planted flowers in her garden. In turn, Harriet taught the children how to knit and told them stories from her childhood. The relationship became special. It was more than just caring for someone in need. Honor added another dimension to their family life.

Adoption helps people feel as though they belong. It meets relational needs that may be missing elsewhere. Adoption can bring joy into a family as people grow and learn together and experience the challenge of adding another person to the family dynamic.

Healing requires change, and some people don't want to change.

---

do we want to be healed?

According to John 5:5-6, one day Jesus walked up to a man who had been sick for thirty-eight years. He asked the man a very strange question: "Do you want to get well?" Why would Jesus ask such a question? Wouldn't anyone want healing? But as we thought about that, we realized that there are some people in life who actually don't want to get well. Healing requires change, and some people don't want to change.

Think about it. If the man got well, he'd probably have to get a job. Instead of having people feel sorry for him all the time and care for him day after day, he'd have to care for himself. Furthermore, he'd probably be expected to care for others. For some, it's better to remain sick than to change. They find it hard to change the way they relate to others, even when those ways are part of the problem. It's easier to moan and complain and blame problems on someone else.

More and more people, though, are seeing the value of honor. It's not only worth the work, but you'll have something valuable to share. Honor changes people. It brings healing to relationships, resolution to conflict, and enjoyment to life. When you share honor with others, you're giving them a gift that will last a lifetime.

take it a step further

1. Read Matthew 5:38-44. Jesus is telling people to do more than what's expected. How does a response of honor help in this kind of difficult situation?

2. Romans 12:10 instructs us to honor each other. Using verses 11-21, make a list of ways that honor can be demonstrated.

3. Read 1 Corinthians 9:19-20. How is this a reflection of honor in relationships?

4. How can honoring others be helpful to the family itself?

TEN

Catch the Vision

We want to close this book by giving you an exciting vision for your family. Yes, you need techniques and specific practical advice, but having all the wisdom in the world is of little value if you don't put it into practice. We want to give you a great way of looking at your family that will affect how you think, speak, and act. This vision for what it means to be an honoring family will challenge you. It challenges us.

It's unfortunate that many who write and speak about the Christian family often limit themselves to drawing on Bible passages that explicitly refer to family relationships. Passages that give instructions to moms, dads, children, brothers, sisters, wives, and husbands are helpful, but they are not the whole story. Many other principles in Scripture apply to everyone, including family members.

In Ephesians 2:19, Paul writes to the church and tells moms, dads, and children an important truth about family life. He tells them that they are part of a bigger family: "Consequently, you are no longer foreigners and aliens, but fellow citizens with God's people and members of God's household." All the members of a Christian family are also members of God's household. One of the ways to stay motivated to honor each other is to view your family as an extension of God's family. The Christian family isn't just a collection of believers living under one roof; it's a spiritual family living under the headship of Christ. Some may object, "But Paul isn't referring to children in the verse. They aren't part of the church, are they?" Interestingly enough, Paul addresses children directly four chapters later when he says, "Children, obey your parents in the Lord." Paul wrote the book with both parents and children in mind as his audience. He's telling them that they're part of a new household with God as the head.

WHeN we recognize that our family
is a part of god's family, we begin
to treat each other differently.

Most Christians know that all believers are part of the family of God. After all, the family metaphor is a common one used to describe our spiritual relationships. But it's amazing how few Christian families practice the ramifications of this. If we're all God's children, what does that make each one of us to each other?

It makes us brothers and sisters. A father is a brother with his son. A daughter is a spiritual sister with her mom, and so on. This perspective on family life adds a tremendous ingredient to our relationships. In fact, when we recognize that our family is a part of God's family, we begin to treat each other differently. We value each other in a special way.

If you ask your children, "Who is the head of our home?" what would they say? Do they understand such a profound truth about the family of God? I (Scott) wanted to bring this idea home to our children, so I asked that question when we were all together. I'd expected them to say, "You are, Dad." I intended to correct them and tell them that God is the head of this family. So I asked them, "Who's the head of this family?" One of the younger children said, "Mom." Another one said, "Yeah, Mom." My ego was struck a little, but I used that opportunity to say, "No, it's not Mom. And it's not me. It's God. He's the head of our household."

Is this just an issue of semantics? No, it's much more than that. In fact, families actually relate differently when they believe that God is the head of the family and that family members are spiritual brothers and sisters to each other.

This truth doesn't remove any sense of responsibility from fathers and mothers to provide leadership in their homes. Leadership is vitally important, but that doesn't make the leader the boss. The Bible teaches that parents have authority in the home and that children are to obey their parents. The Bible also teaches that husbands have an initiating role with their wives and that wives have a responding role with their husbands. But that's not all there is in a biblical view of the family. Parents who stop there miss some of the richness of family life, and the real losers are the children. Parents who overemphasize authority and role definition often end up with families that may look good to others but are missing a key ingredient—honor. It's only a matter of time before the real truth comes out and the family is exposed for what it really is.

So What Is a Christian Family Anyway?

There is a definition of the Christian family that may be a little different than what you're used to. It's certainly refreshing to many:

the christian family

> A collection of earthly parents and children who have been adopted into the household of God by faith, thus becoming spiritual brothers and sisters with God as their Father.

Being God's family must be our primary identity. Once when Jesus was ministering at someone's home, a person came up to him and said, "'Your mother and brothers are standing outside, wanting to speak to you.' [Jesus] replied to him, 'Who is my mother, and who are my brothers?' Pointing to his disciples, he said, 'Here are my mother and my brothers. For whoever does the will of my Father in heaven is my brother and sister and mother'" (Matthew 12:47-50). With these words, Jesus is demonstrating the priority of our spiritual relationships in God's family.

To be in God's family is more important than what your family name is or what country your ancestors came from. Your children are your brothers and sisters in Christ. They may not have been in the family as long as you have, but you need to respect what God is doing in their hearts and lives. God relates to them directly, as well as through you, their parents.

But what about those passages that talk about the roles and responsibilities in the family? Let's go back and look at them for a moment. If you take time to look at the context of each of those passages, you'll find that the greater context supports a mutual spiritual relationship to one another.

In Ephesians 5:22–6:4, for example, wives are instructed to submit to their husbands, husbands are directed to love their wives, and children are commanded to obey their parents. But look at the verse just before. It says, "Submit to one another out of reverence for Christ." In fact, chapters 4 and 5 are full of instructions that will guide all family members toward successful relationships.

Colossians 3:18-21 talks about family roles and gives specific instructions to husbands, wives, and children. In the verses just preceding them, instructions are given for everyone to be kind, humble, gentle and patient, forgiving, and putting on love, which provides unity.

In 1 Peter 3:1-7 instructions are given to husbands and wives, but in verse 8, Peter says, "Finally, all of you, live in harmony with one another; be sympathetic, love as brothers, be compassionate and humble." Even the passages that define the importance of roles in family life are surrounded by instructions emphasizing mutual honor.

It would be foolish to deny the importance of the earthly family in God's kingdom program. After all, as Jesus was dying on the cross, he told his mother that she should take the apostle John as her son, and he should take her as his mother (John 19:26-27). Here, at the very end of his life, Jesus gave her special attention because she was still his mother. He had not disowned her.

However, before we slap our hands together and end the conversation, we must also consider another story. When Jesus was twelve years old, he spent three days in the temple courts discussing religious matters with the teachers while his parents were anxiously trying to find him. Mary wasn't too pleased. When challenged, Jesus said, "Didn't you know I had to be in my Father's house?" (Luke 2:49).

Viewing our family as an extension of God's family provides a leveling effect. We're all sinners needing equal grace, and each member is surrendering to the same Lord. Every day we fail and must confess our sin to the Father. Rather than looking for power over one another, we must learn mutual humility, acceptance, admonition, and love. Overemphasizing roles leads to feelings of obligation and duty. Viewing the family as a subset of God's family helps people feel a part of a team, with honor providing a tight bond.

children Are expensive

What happens when you look at your children as brothers and sisters in Christ? You value them for who they are, recognizing God's work in them. Parents sometimes view their children as projects, not people. It's been said, "The only thing you can take with you to heaven is your kids." By viewing them as brothers and sisters, you add a helpful dimension to family life.

One woman had a table worth $600. She valued the table but decided to sell it and set the price at $400. A man came to purchase the table and liked it very much. He offered her $300. The woman explained to the man that the table was worth $600 and that she couldn't reduce the price any more. The woman felt as if she had reduced the price too much already.

The man thought about it and said, "Lady, we would both be happy if you would just change the price." The woman knew the man was right. So she went back to the price tag, crossed out "$400" and wrote "$600." The man was shocked. The woman said, "The table is worth $600."

"But it costs so much."

The woman was focusing on the table's value; the man was looking at the cost. Parents often do this with their children. Raising children has a high price tag. It includes loss of sleep and fewer choices for your free time and money. It means transporting them from here to there and back again. Children cost much more than parents ever imagined. But if you focus too much on the cost, you lose sight of the value. Parents who realize the value of their children conduct themselves differently. Closeness is the result.

The man valued the table, so he bought it. He took it home and put it in a special place. If anyone put a drink down, he quickly provided a coaster, wanting to protect that table. Why? He knew its value. It was worth a lot to him.

WHEN WE RECOGNIZE A PERSON'S VALUE,
IT'S EASY TO GIVE HIM OR HER HONOR.

Children aren't possessions; they're treasures. Most parents don't realize what they're getting into when they bring that little bundle of cuteness home from the hospital. They may get irritated or lose some of the joy of parenting over the years. Part of the solution is to get your mind off the cost and onto the value of your children. They are, or will be, brothers and sisters in Christ. When we recognize a person's value, it's easy to give him or her honor.

This view of the earthly family being a subset of God's family has some tremendous ramifications. Singles are no longer without a family. Special needs children are no longer the responsibility of just one family. Infertile couples are not really childless. We can love earthly family members without needing their support and approval. We don't spend our lives trying in vain to please our family. We now please our heavenly Father instead, freeing us to give honor to others. Even if unbelievers live in your home—or your children have not committed themselves to the faith as you have—the rules for successful relationships are the same. God's principles for success in his church will work in any home. Train your children to live as brothers and sisters in Christ. If they haven't yet embraced the faith, they will see the benefits of doing so through your example and teaching.

Some who read these words will shake their heads and say, "Yes, but you don't know my children. They aren't ready for this yet." And maybe they aren't. But being an honoring family means growing into this reality. The goal is to grow together as a part of God's family in ways you haven't done before.

Maintaining a delicate balance

The family is complex. Each individual thinks and acts independently, yet all family members are attached, relating and adjusting themselves to each other. It's like a delicate mobile; each thread holds the whole structure in a careful balance. In the same way, honor creates a balance that holds the family together and allows it to withstand the winds of adversity. Honor weaves through a family, eventually ending up with one united strand of honor going up to God. If honor is missing in a family, then the balance isn't there. Many family mobiles are tied up in knots or hanging precariously. They need to regain balance in their family life, and although difficult problems may need to be addressed, it all starts with honor.

Parents often look to their children's future and set aside a nest egg for college or other special needs. But one of the best investments a parent can make has nothing to do with money. It has to do with honor. The daily work of building a home where honor reigns pays huge dividends in the end. It takes diligence, perseverance, and even a little creativity, but the results speak for themselves.

You need a vision for your family that will change the way you think, feel, and act toward each other. It's a vision for parents, but it's a vision for children as well. It's amazing when a husband and wife actually come to the understanding that they're brother and sister in Christ. It's even more exciting when parents recognize that this same truth applies to their children. But the most exciting is when children recognize that their parents are really their spiritual brothers and sisters.

In the movie *Hook,* a spin-off of the *Peter Pan* story, the Lost Boys spent hour after hour trying to help Robin Williams understand that he was more than a high-profile lawyer. He was, in reality, Peter Pan. When the reality finally took hold, and his daughter saw him flying through the air, she realized with wonder and amazement that her dad really was Peter Pan.

That same thing can happen in your family. Look past your roles as fathers and mothers, lawyers and businessmen, homemakers and sports fans, children and students, and discover who you really are. You're children of God through faith in his Son. Your life is now characterized by honor. Each day you look for ways to show it to others. Your children will see the difference and exclaim with gladness, "My dad and my mom know how to honor!" And they will want to grow in honor too!

take it a step further

1. How can you emphasize your own "brother-sister" relationship with your children without weakening your authority in the home?

2. What differences take place in a family when they view themselves as an extension of God's family?

3. What understanding about God freed Jesus to respond with grace in a difficult situation in 1 Peter 2:21-23? How can that understanding of God help us to show honor?

APPENDIX

family together times focused on Honor

These eight interactive discussions and activities are focused on honor and designed for the whole family.

Family discussions focused on honor can do much to develop it as a lifestyle. The following activities are designed with families in mind. They are fun and insightful ways to get parents and children engaged in helpful discussions about honor.

You can use these activities with children of all ages. Teens as well as young children benefit from times of discussion and activities related to honor. The older the child, the deeper the dialogue you'll be able to have. If you have a large age span in your children, you may have to adapt the material, but it's generally best to target the older children and let the younger ones learn what they can.

These family times are designed to be short (fifteen to twenty minutes) and are best followed by a positive family experience like going out to eat, playing a game, or spending an evening together. It's important to avoid making these sessions discipline times, although the things learned here may open doors for further discipline in the course of the week. Family Together Times are meant to be enjoyable for all members of the family.

Suggestions for getting the most out of family together times

Sometimes parents approach family meetings or group discussions with fear and trepidation. Others approach the time with unrealistic expectations. Here are some suggestions for getting the most out of Family Together Times.

Choose a time when the family is not overly tired or hungry. Allow children to be children. They may become silly at times, wiggle or fidget, or give strange answers to the questions you're asking. Teens may be quiet or try to be funny. Although you will probably do some gentle correction, be careful not to demand too much, thus making this a negative experience. You want your children to enjoy these times and look forward to them.

Each Family Together Time is divided into five parts. The *preparation* will help you get everything ready. The *review* section reminds the family of previous lessons. The *introduction* can be read to the family or summarized, tailoring it to your specific needs. *A lesson from God's Word* contains a scripture passage to read and teaching ideas. Children may want to use their own Bibles. Help them find the verse, and encourage them to read it. The *application* activity is designed to bring the truth to life. Have fun, and use the activity to teach the concept. Words in italics in the instructions are meant for you, the leader. The other words may be read out loud to your family.

Questions help children get involved and process what they're hearing. A number of questions have been suggested, and their answers could take you on a variety of tangents. In fact, you may find that you start in one place and end up somewhere unexpected. Pick and choose the questions according to the needs of your family. Adapt them to make them more age appropriate if necessary. If one question doesn't seem to be working, go on to another.

Keep the goal in mind: helping your family grow in the area of honor. Try to communicate the main truth in several ways. Some Family Together Times will be more productive than others. When you're done with a session, you may feel disappointed because of the silliness, or you may feel the message didn't get through. Don't get discouraged. You are planting seeds for future growth, and children often absorb more than parents realize. A healthy family can flex with the different moods and challenges of Family Together Times.

family together time #1:
An introduction to Honor

Goal

To introduce the concept of honor and the fact that every person is valuable

Preparation

Gather the following: a dinner plate, a large glass of water, a pepper shaker, and a small amount of dish soap in a bowl (the secret ingredient).

Introduction

Relationships are like the water in this plate. *Fill the plate with water almost to its edge.* But relationships can be quite a challenge at times. All kinds of negative things happen, and people get hurt and become distant from each other. *Sprinkle pepper onto the water, illustrating the conflict that can take place in relationships.* When that happens, people aren't happy, and others aren't happy with them. The relationships aren't close or clear anymore.

I have a secret ingredient here, though, that will help clear up the relationship. What I want you to see is that adding one thing can make a big difference. *Dip your finger into the bowl of soap and then dip it into the side of the dish. All the pepper will move to the opposite side.* We call this a secret ingredient because of what it does when you add it to the water.

The same thing is true in family relationships. Today I want to share with you a very special quality. If you take time to learn this and put it into practice, you will see that your life is much easier and that others find you much more enjoyable to be around. You will be amazed at how relationships will change. Most people don't have this quality and don't practice it, but when you do, you will see some very interesting results. The secret ingredient for relationships is honor.

A Lesson from God's Word

Turn in your Bible to Romans 12:10. "Honor one another above yourselves." The word *honor* means to value someone. This verse tells us to honor other people above ourselves. God has given to us his success principles in his Word, the Bible. When we put those principles into practice, then we can be joyful and can bring joy to others as well.

Honor is the secret ingredient for relationships. Just like the ingredient in the dish, honor can clear up problems in the family. We will talk about honor for the next several weeks, but today I want you to understand one important thing about honor. It means that we value others and treat them as special.

Let's talk about valuable things for a moment. If we had to leave our house to move to another place and couldn't take our belongings with us, which one of your things would you choose to take with you? *Let every member of the family share what they would take.*

How do we treat the things we value? *Add the following answers if they aren't otherwise contributed to the conversation:* We are careful about the way we handle them. We take extra time to care for them properly. We are gentle instead of rough. We try to prevent anything bad from happening to them.

Honor is the way we treat something that is special. We honor things that we value. When you learn to value other people in relationships, then good things happen. You are careful about the way you speak or act around those people. You become gentle with them and take time to care for them properly. You look for ways to make good things rather than bad things happen in your relationship. Here is a two-part story to illustrate this. We'll read one part this week and the rest next time.

Life in the Pierson Family

"I think you're doing that step backward," Bill said as he watched his friend Clark pull the rope through the loop.

"Okay, how about I bring it around this way and put it through here?" Clark asked.

"Yeah, that's the way." Bill had invited his friend Clark over for the day. Both boys were eleven years old and were eager to learn how to duplicate the knots on the Boy Scout knot board. They wanted to learn how each knot could be used in different ways for different jobs.

"Hey, Bill, let's put on some music," Clark suggested as he went over to the CD rack in Bill's room. Clark began opening the CDs and checking out the different kinds of music.

Bill continued to work with the knots but also kept a close eye on Clark. He didn't want his CDs damaged and knew that one scratch could mean he'd have to replace that CD.

Bill's mom passed by the bedroom. "Bill, I want you and Clark to please go down and clean up Dad's tools that you left on the back patio."

"Oh, Mom, do we have to do it now?" Bill said with an irritated voice.

Mom sighed, her disappointment evident on her face. "Yes, Bill, please go clean it up now." It seemed that whenever Bill was asked to do something, no matter how nicely, he would grumble and complain.

Bill and Clark went down and cleaned up the tools. As Bill was putting the hammer in the shed, Clark returned to the bedroom.

When Bill walked back into his room, he was surprised to see several of his CDs lying on the bed. "What are you doing?"

"I was just getting out a couple of CDs for us to listen to," replied Clark.

"Well don't lay them down that way! They have to be face up. I've already lost some of my good ones. If you want to use something, ask me, and I'll get it for you."

Clark was taken aback by Bill's reaction. He handed the CDs to Bill, who put on some music. They both began working with the knots again.

That evening at devotions Dad read the verse from Romans 12:10: "Honor one another above yourselves." Dad explained, "This word *honor* means to value something. It means that you show value to other people and treat them kindly or with respect. What's something you have that you think is pretty valuable?"

As they went around the table, each person shared something that was especially important to him or her. Mom valued the family photo album. Dad really liked his new power drill.

When it was Bill's turn, he said, "I like my CDs." He thought for a moment and then added slowly, "Today Clark and I were playing in my room, and Clark took a couple of my CDs out. He wasn't very careful, and I got angry with him. I guess I was valuing my CDs, but I wasn't valuing Clark. Maybe I could've been easier on him."

Mom looked thoughtfully across the table at Bill. "You know, Bill, I've been feeling hurt by the way you treat *me* sometimes too, especially when I give you an instruction."

"What do you mean?" Bill asked.

"Well, when I asked you and Clark to clean up the tools this afternoon, you grumbled and were unkind to me. And earlier today, when I asked you to help clean up after breakfast, you did the same thing. I've noticed that when I ask you to do something, you often respond to me with an angry look or unkind words."

Bill was surprised. He recognized what his mom said was true. He hadn't even realized it before. "Okay," was all Bill could say.

Dad continued, "I know that sometimes I get harsh with my partner at work. It's not because she did anything wrong, but it's often because I'm under pressure, and I take it out on her. I've also noticed that when people in the office aren't feeling very good, sometimes I can brighten everyone's day with my attitude and the way I treat others. It's amazing what honor can do. I need to work on this idea of honoring others more. Why don't we all think about honor this week and report back next week with the results?"

The Pierson family agreed that they would all work on honor in the coming week and report back the next week about how it was going. Dad closed their time in prayer, and then Mom said, "Anybody want some ice cream?" Everyone was eager to enjoy a special dessert together.

Application

What does *honor* mean? It means that we show we value someone else. What are some ways we can value Mom this week? What are some ways that we can show we value Dad this week? What are some ways that we can show we value _____ (*list each person in the family to make this very practical and personal*) this week? *Include answers like, say thank you, share toys, give a hug, don't be easily irritated, etc. Close with prayer and the hopeful attitude that your family will be different this week because of honor.*

family together time #2:
what is Honor Anyway?

Goal

To help the family understand that honor is a gift, to feel the joy of giving, and to look for ways to give honor in family life with a focus on gratefulness

Preparation

Wrap one gift for each member of your family. Each gift should contain two pieces of candy, one to keep and one to give away. Gift-wrap a small baggie of dirt. Ask the family to come together and bring their Bibles. For a treat you might want to buy some special cookies like the ones mentioned in the story.

Review

Last week we learned about a secret ingredient. Does anyone remember what it was? Honor is a secret ingredient for relationships. What did we learn last week was another word for honor? *Value.*

Can you think of any ways that someone showed you honor or you showed honor this week?

Introduction

Here are some different ways the word *honor* is used. What does the word mean in each of these contexts: honor student, guest of honor, honor roll, Your Honor, honor system, on your honor? Can you think of more ways that the word *honor* is used? *Choose only a few of these honor phrases, depending on the age of your family, so you don't lose their interest.*

With these words in mind, how would you summarize what honor means?

Why do parents put bumper stickers on their cars that say that their child is an honor student?

For older children: Do you think honoring children for good grades is a good idea? Why or why not? *Teens may like to discuss the advantages and disadvantages of giving someone honor for good grades.*

A Lesson from God's Word

There are many verses in the Scriptures that talk about honor. Let's read one of them, Proverbs 15:33: "The fear of the LORD teaches a man wisdom, and humility comes before honor." Why do you think the Bible says humility comes before honor? *When people recognize their need for others and the importance of others in their lives, then they have an attitude that causes others to want to honor them. With younger children you might just talk about the value of humility and what it is.*

One of the ways we can honor people is by being grateful for the things they do. How do you think gratefulness and honor might be related? *Gratefulness is a way of honoring someone who has done something for you.*

Listen as I read the rest of the story of the Pierson family.

"Bill…Margaret…," Dad called, "Mom's home from the store. Let's help bring in the groceries."

"Dad, I'm working on my baseball cards," Bill called from his bedroom. "Do I have to come now?"

"Yes, Bill, I want you to come and give us a hand. Help carry in the groceries, and then you can go back to your baseball cards."

Bill reluctantly left his bedroom and went to help Margaret, Dad, and Mom bring the groceries into the house.

"It's not easy shopping for this family," Dad told the children. "The least we can do is help bring in the bags."

As Bill was bringing in the last bag, Mom said, "Thanks for your help." She smiled and looked into one of the bags. "Now where is it? I know it's here somewhere. Bill, let me see that bag."

Bill plopped the bag on the table, and Mom looked inside. "Here we go. A treat for everyone."

Bill's mouth began to water as he realized Mom had bought cookies with chocolate frosting and mint filling. They were his favorite kind. "Oh good. I love these cookies!" Bill exclaimed. Mom handed him the bag, and he went right to work, opening it, and sticking the first cookie into his mouth.

"I want one too," Margaret said as she reached for a cookie and popped it into her mouth.

Mom began putting away groceries while Bill and Margaret took the cookies out to the porch.

Dad watched them walk away with their treat. He noticed that neither of the children had said "thank you" to their mother, and he determined to talk about this at their together time that evening.

"Who remembers what the secret ingredient is for relationships?" Dad asked as they all gathered in the living room after dinner.

"Honor," Margaret said.

"Yes, that's right," replied Dad, "and what is another word for honor that we talked about?"

"Value," Bill replied.

"Good. Can you think of any ways that you showed honor this week or that someone showed honor to you?" Dad asked.

The children were quiet. Although he didn't show it, Dad was disappointed. He had hoped they would catch a vision for honor and look for ways to demonstrate it.

"I felt honored when you took me out to dinner the other night, honey," Mom said to Dad.

"Thanks, I enjoyed it too," Dad said with a smile. "What about you, Bill? Last week you mentioned that you had a problem with Clark and were harsh with him. Have you thought any more about that?"

"Oh, yeah. I remember now," Bill said. "I told Clark I was sorry the next day, and we worked it out."

"That's good," said Dad. "The way we treat each other is very important, and honor can actually be the secret ingredient. We also talked about that last week as well. I've got an idea for all of us for this week," Dad continued. "One of the ways to show honor is to express gratefulness to others. Can you think of something someone has done for you lately that makes you feel grateful?"

Margaret was quiet for a moment, then her eyes lit up. "I liked it when Mom made pancakes this morning for breakfast," she said.

"That's a good example, Margaret. Did you say thank you to Mom?"

"Well, no, I guess I didn't."

"I noticed Mom brought home a treat from the store today. Was anyone grateful for that?" Dad asked.

"Yeah, those cookies were great, Mom. Thanks!" Bill said.

"You're welcome. I'm glad you liked them."

"There are lots of ways to say thank you to each other besides using those words," Dad said. "Can you think of any?"

"You could give the person a card," Margaret said.

"You could give a hug and say 'I love you,'" Bill added.

"Those are good ideas," Dad said. "Another thing you can do is help someone. If you're grateful that Mom makes pancakes, maybe you could take time to clear the table afterward. Or when she goes shopping for our family, we could all help bring in the groceries."

Mom thought for a moment and then added, "It reminds me of that story in the Bible where Jesus healed ten lepers but only one came back to say thank you. Jesus asked him, 'Where are the other nine?' I don't think Jesus wanted the recognition for healing them, but he knew that saying thank you is not only helpful to the person hearing it; it also does something for the person who says it."

"Here's what I'd like us to do this week," Dad said. "One of the ways families can honor each other is by being grateful. I'd like each of us to come to dinner every night this week and share one time we expressed gratefulness to someone that day. It could be anyone and any creative way."

Everyone agreed to give it a try, and Dad was hopeful that tomorrow night at dinner he'd hear a good report.

Application

One way to show honor is by giving a gift. I have a gift here that I would like to give someone in this family. *Present the dirt gift, but keep the other gifts hidden. Choose one child. You may want to choose an older child who enjoys a joke, or open the gift yourself if you think it may be overly embarrassing to your children.*

Before the present is opened, ask the family: How do you feel when you get a gift? That's how you feel when someone honors you. I'm going to give _____ a gift, and then we'll ask how he or she feels. *Give the gift of dirt to open. Ask,* How does it make you feel when you open a present and you get dirt? Really terrible, I bet. That's how people feel when they are treated in dishonoring ways.

The family is a place where honor can be given. It helps the family work more smoothly. When we show dishonor, it's like giving a gift of dirt.

What are ways we dishonor each other in the family? *Fighting, bickering, a me-first attitude, interrupting, etc.* I really do want to honor you today, so I've brought you each a gift. I have some instructions to go with this gift. The gift has two parts—one part to keep and the other to give away. You can give it to anyone else to show honor to that person. Giving honor is like giving a gift.

Hand out the gifts to each member of your family, and allow everyone to open them as you restate the instruction: One part is to keep, and the other part is to give away.

An important way to show honor is to tell people what you appreciate about them. Gratefulness and praise are gifts that show honor. Let's end our time tonight with every person thinking of one thing to thank God for, and then we'll close in prayer.

Spend a few minutes praying together as a family. Remind your children that talking to God can be short and simple. You may want to allow each child to share one thing he or she appreciates about God, or you may want to let your children thank God for your family. Close the prayer after a few minutes, and then thank your children for their participation.

fдmilY togetHer timе #3:
HoNoriNg Leдderſ

Goal

To help the family understand that one can choose to honor any leader and to help individuals practice showing honor to a leader even if they have a better idea or different ways to do things

Preparation

Choose one child ahead of time to be honored. This can be especially fun if you choose a younger child but one who is still able to give directions. Explain that as part of the Family Together Time you are going to let him or her be the boss and everyone else will be the servants. The assignment will be to clean out the car (or clean out a shed or closet or some other ten- to twenty-minute task). Ask that child to think about different assignments they will give each member of the family in order to get the task done. Prepare a special dessert to enjoy at the conclusion of this session.

Call people together, and have them bring their Bibles.

Review

Who remembers what honor is? *Use this time to review the previous session. Point out that honor is a gift that can come in a number of forms.*

Can anyone think of a time you felt honored this week?

Introduction

We are going to talk about honoring leaders or people in authority. What are some examples of the different kinds of leaders and authority figures that we must listen to or obey? *Examples should include ones from government, school, church, and home.*

A Lesson from God's Word

Let's read what the Bible has to say about honoring leaders. *Read Romans 13:1-7:*

> Everyone must submit himself to the governing authorities, for there is no authority except that which God has established. The authorities that exist have been established by God. Consequently, he who rebels against the authority is rebelling against what God has instituted, and those who do so will bring judgment on themselves. For rulers hold no terror for those who do right, but for those who do wrong. Do you want to be free from fear of the one in authority? Then do what is right and he will commend you. For he is God's servant to do you good. But if you do wrong, be afraid, for he does not bear the sword for nothing. He is God's servant, an agent of wrath to bring punishment on the wrongdoer. Therefore, it is necessary to submit to the authorities, not only because of possible punishment but also because of conscience.
>
> This is also why you pay taxes, for the authorities are God's servants, who give their full time to governing. Give everyone

what you owe him: If you owe taxes, pay taxes; if revenue, then revenue; if respect, then respect; if honor, then honor.

Who is to be honored in this passage? Why do we honor them? How do you show honor when you disagree with the leader or wish the leader would lead in a different way?

For older children: How do you show honor to a president or elected official you think is the wrong person for the position? *Teens might find it interesting to discuss the value of honoring a teacher, coach, or other leader whom they don't like. It's especially challenging to know how to talk about that person in an honoring way.*

Just because someone is in authority doesn't mean that person has the best ideas or is somehow superior. Someone has to be the leader, and for one reason or another, that person is it. Those who are not leaders have the job of supporting the leader and helping to accomplish the goal. Is there an honoring way to disagree with a leader? Is there an honoring way to suggest an idea or point out a better way to lead? Is it ever okay to tell a leader that he or she is doing something wrong?

For older children: What is the difference between honor and respect? Sometimes we respect a person's position. What extra does honor give?

The following ideas are suggestions for further discussion with older children: We honor leaders first of all because God can work in our lives through earthly leaders. Leaders have responsibility to direct the affairs of organizations, countries, and even families. Their tasks are difficult, and their responsibilities are complicated. Hard decisions have to be made, and people are inevitably offended. But leaders are human. They make mistakes and struggle with emotions and issues just like anyone else.

God wants us to honor leaders not just because they make good decisions or because they deserve our honor. We honor leaders because it does something for us as well. When Johnny has a tyrant for a soccer coach, how should he respond? Can Johnny honor the coach? If he does, he will grow and mature in some valuable ways himself.

Addressing leaders with gracious speech and a good attitude are ways to honor them. You can disagree, and you may voice your opinion, but there's a big difference between someone who voices an opinion in an obnoxious way and a person who tries to motivate change in a supportive way.

Sometimes, simply sharing an alternative or pointing out what may be a mistake can be helpful. It's important to consider the attitude, timing, and situation. Challenging a leader in the right way can be a valuable means of learning honor because of the potential for dishonor. The primary lesson learned is that disagreement doesn't warrant dishonoring speech or actions.

Application

Today I have asked _____ to be our leader. We are all going to practice honoring our leader while he *(or she)* leads us in cleaning the car *(or other task)*. Our leader has been developing a plan and is ready to go. So I'm now going to pass the leadership on.

During the activity, be a servant, and even play along in some dra-

matic ways. You may want to start whining and complaining and then say, "Oh, that's not honoring." Say, "I disagree with that," and then say, "Let me try that again." Look for ways to support the leader with humility by asking questions to direct the leader's decisions. Make it a fun time by playacting some of the difficult leader-follower issues.

After the activity take time to debrief about how people felt, including the leader.

What are some ways you were able to show honor to the leader? What is the right thing to do when it's hard to show honor? What's hard about leading? What's hard about following?

Being a leader and being a follower are difficult at times. We can all get STRESSED. *Write that word on a piece of paper.*

We're going to have a treat now, and what it is, is hidden in this word. Turn this word around, and spell it backward, and what do you have? DESSERTS.

End with prayer.

family together time #4:
Honoring parents

Goal

To help the family realize that one way to show honor is to do more than what's expected. Each child will be able to enjoy bringing delight to a parent by giving a surprise.

Preparation

Choose some chores that take less than five minutes and are easy to accomplish. Write each assignment on an index card. Choose simple tasks such as refilling the salt shaker, straightening the towels in the bathroom, or organizing the bookshelf.

Plan a special activity afterward, like a trip to the park, a sleepover with friends, or a night making goodies in the kitchen.

Review

What is one thing you remember from our discussion last week about honoring leaders? Tell about a time someone was leading this week and you tried to follow with honor. Did you see any dishonor to leaders this week? *Be careful about being overly critical of your children here. Making this a time of discipline will weaken the potential for discussion.*

Introduction

Today we're going to talk about how children can honor their parents and what rewards come when they do. Let's all honor Mom for a moment *(or Dad)*. Let's go around and have each person tell something he or she appreciates about what Mom does for us. Next let's go around and tell one thing we admire about Mom. *Appreciation focuses on behavior. Admiration focuses on character.* Telling those things to Mom is a way of honoring her.

A Lesson from God's Word

Read Ephesians 6:2-3: "'Honor your father and mother'—which is the first commandment with a promise—'that it may go well with you and that you may enjoy long life on the earth.'"

What does it mean to honor parents?

Don't let the discussion end by simply suggesting that honor is accomplished by obeying. There are other ways to show honor that involve attitude, thinking of what pleases the other person, and doing more than what's expected.

What is the promise mentioned in this verse? Why do you think that children who give honor enjoy life? As in the example earlier of honoring Mom, honor makes others feel good too, including the one showing honor. Honor makes life more enjoyable for everyone.

Application

One of the ways to honor parents is to do more than what's expected. When an instruction is given for you to obey—and you do it—that's obedience. When you go an extra step, that's honor. For example, if I were to ask you to pick up the toys in your room and you also organize the toy shelf, that would be extra and would be honoring. We are going to practice that today and give you an opportunity to show honor to _____ *(Mom or Dad)*.

We have assignments for each person. Your job is to complete the assignment and then get it checked by Mom or Dad. Before you get it checked, I want you to do something extra. You choose what that extra is. Do more than what's expected. Think about something that would please _____ *(Mom or Dad)*. The extra you do is showing honor. Then let's see how _____ *(Mom or Dad)* responds when you report back.

Hand out the cards with simple tasks on them. Be sure to have the children report back. When you inspect their work, show delight at the extra thing each child did. If you can't tell what they did extra, ask them, and then offer praise. Your delight is their reward. You may want to have fun with this by exaggerating your delight.

After the activity, debrief about how people felt. Let people share what extra thing they did and talk about how it feels when Mom or Dad is delighted. Honor can be quite fun because it brings joy to life.

Thank you for honoring us in this activity. I also want to honor you, so I would like to take you out tonight. *Watch for delight. Point it out. Ask them,* Do you feel honored? *Ask that each family member show honor to others this week so that everyone can be delighted to be in the family.*

End with prayer.

family together time #5:
checking out the Attitude

Goal

To know that attitude reveals the heart and that when family members understand honor, it's reflected in their attitudes

Preparation

Make a poster to hang up that defines honor this way: Honor is treating people as special, doing more than what's expected, and having a good attitude. Make a second poster that reads: Three opportunities for demonstrating a good attitude: when being corrected, when receiving an instruction, and when receiving a no answer.

Review

Last time we talked about how honor can be demonstrated by doing more than what's expected. What does it look like when Dad is delighted? Someone pretend to be Dad when he is honored by your doing more than he asked. How does Mom look when she is honored?

Can you think of a time this week when you or someone else did more than was expected? If your job was to feed the dog and you wanted to show honor, what extra thing might you do? If you had an English assignment to turn in at school, how might you do more than what's expected? Doing more than what's expected is part of the honor definition. *Bring out your poster of the honor definition, and decide as a family where to put it.*

Introduction

Today we're going to talk about the last part of that honor definition, having a good attitude. What does a bad attitude look like? *Draw out as many symptoms as you can. This is important because it helps people see, in real terms, that behaviors demonstrate what's going on in the heart. Include nonverbal cues like pouting, crossed arms, looking down, and sticking out the bottom lip. Also include verbal cues like grunting, clicking the tongue, a sharp tone of voice, and sarcasm. Don't focus on just your children's symptoms. Help them see the symptoms of bad attitudes in others as well.*

Do Dad and Mom ever demonstrate a bad attitude? What does that look like? *Your transparency will provide teaching opportunities as well as the recognition that everyone in the family is learning honor.*

A Lesson from God's Word

Let's look at a Bible passage and see a man who had a bad attitude. I'm going to read the verses and then I'm going to ask, "How could you tell that the man had a bad attitude?"

Adam lay with his wife Eve, and she became pregnant and gave birth to Cain. She said, "With the help of the LORD I have brought forth a man." Later she gave birth to his brother Abel.

Now Abel kept flocks, and Cain worked the soil. In the

course of time Cain brought some of the fruits of the soil as an offering to the LORD. But Abel brought fat portions from some of the firstborn of his flock. The LORD looked with favor on Abel and his offering, but on Cain and his offering he did not look with favor. So Cain was very angry, and his face was downcast.

Then the LORD said to Cain, "Why are you angry? Why is your face downcast? If you do what is right, will you not be accepted? But if you do not do what is right, sin is crouching at your door; it desires to have you, but you must master it."

Now Cain said to his brother Abel, "Let's go out to the field." And while they were in the field, Cain attacked his brother Abel and killed him.

Then the LORD said to Cain, "Where is your brother Abel?"

"I don't know," he replied. "Am I my brother's keeper?"

The LORD said, "What have you done? Listen! Your brother's blood cries out to me from the ground. Now you are under a curse and driven from the ground, which opened its mouth to receive your brother's blood from your hand. When you work the ground, it will no longer yield its crops for you. You will be a restless wanderer on the earth." (Genesis 4:1-12)

How could you tell that Cain had a bad attitude? Let's see each person make a downcast face. *Make this a fun time as each person pouts or looks mean or sad.*

Cain was sarcastic in verse 9. What are some examples of sarcasm? Sarcasm is when the tone of voice carries a different meaning than the words imply. *If this is a problem in your family, you might spend extra time giving examples and then talking about how sarcasm can be a symptom of a bad attitude. This is especially helpful for teenagers. You might continue the dialogue with a discussion about whether sarcasm is always wrong.*

Bring out your second poster. The most common areas where children have bad attitudes are these: when receiving an instruction, when being corrected, and when receiving a no answer. This poster will help us remember those three areas this week. *Decide where you will place this poster in the house.*

Application

We're going to try a role-play game. I will read you part of a story, and we'll role-play the end of it, showing both a good and a bad attitude. *These stories have examples for parents as well as children. You may find it fun to allow children to role-play the parent illustrations and the parents to role-play the child illustrations. Also, one person might demonstrate a good attitude and then another a bad attitude.*

Story #1. It's Dad's turn to do the dinner dishes. The football game is about to start, and he walks into the kitchen to get a soda. He sees the messy kitchen and realizes that he had agreed to clean up before he relaxed for the evening. He knows that now is the time to do the dishes. How might he respond if he has a bad attitude? How might he respond if he has a good attitude?

Story #2. Billy, age eight, sees his friend eating an ice cream cone. He wants one too, but it's 5:00 P.M. He goes into the house and nicely asks Mom if he can have some ice cream. Mom says,

"No, we're eating dinner in half an hour." How might Billy respond with a bad attitude? How might he respond with a good attitude?

Story #3. It's 8:00 P.M., and Mom is tired and wants to read and rest for a while. Her teenage daughter, Sara, comes in with a problem. "Mom, I thought I had what I need for my homework, but I left my science book over at Karen's house this afternoon. Could you please drive me over there to get it? Mom knows that Sara's request is reasonable (unless this happens all the time). How might she respond with a bad attitude? How might she respond with a good attitude?

Story #4. Kelly is fourteen years old. Dad comes into her room and says, "Kelly, I asked you to mow the lawn this week, and now it's Saturday, and the lawn hasn't been done. I'd like you please to mow it before you spend time with friends this afternoon." How might Kelly respond with a bad attitude? How might she respond with a good attitude?

Review the two posters, and ask the family to demonstrate honor in their attitudes this week. Close in prayer.

family together time #6:
the subtle messages
behind the words

Goal

To understand that communication involves more than words and it's often the unspoken cues that communicate honor or dishonor to others

Preparation

Prepare three sets of cards. The first set contains several simple instructions. For example, "Move a chair from the dining room to the kitchen." "Mom and daughter switch seats." "Lie on the floor." "Stand up, turn around, and sit down." "Clap your hands three times." "Bring me a book." "Give Dad a glass of water." "Open the front door." "Turn the light off." "Pick up your brother, and put him on the couch." These simple requests will be used as part of a game later.

The second set of cards should each contain one of the following sentences. "I can't believe she's doing it again." "My car wheel fell off." "There's food on the table." "The football game is starting." "Grandma's on her way up the walk." "Jack, do you know where my brush is?" "The movie has been postponed till five o'clock." "Grades are coming out next week." "The lights are on in the basement." "Our whole family will be home over the weekend."

Each of the third set of cards should contain one of the following emotion words: "excited," "irritated," "angry," "happy," "sad."

Review

Last time we talked about the importance of attitude. Can someone tell us about a time when you tried to have a good attitude even though you felt like having a bad attitude? If you're starting to have a bad attitude and you want to have a good one, what do you say to yourself to make the switch?

Introduction

Today we're going to talk about messages that we give to others. Messages often contain words but not always. There are other ways we communicate messages as well. We're going to play a game, using cues other than words to communicate a message. I have several cards here that have instructions on them. I would like you to take one card, read it to yourself, and then instruct someone to do the task on the card, but you can't use any words. *Use card set #1. Let several, if not all, people act out in charade fashion the request in order to get the person to do the task.*

We communicate things to people in ways other than words. Posture, gestures, and facial expressions are just a few. Honor can be communicated in a number of ways without words. In fact, you might *do* what Mom says in order to obey her but dishonor her in the *way* you do it.

A Lesson from God's Word

What is your favorite kind of food? *Allow everyone to answer.* Do you like Mexican food or Indian food? Why? These kinds of foods are spicy, and people either like them or not, but many foods are seasoned. *Talk about seasonings that people like.* Let's read Colossians 4:6: "Let your conversation be always full of grace, seasoned with salt, so that you may know how to answer everyone." What does it mean to have a conversation that is seasoned with salt?

You might want to have some popcorn or pretzels with salt and some without and talk about how seasoning affects the food we eat.

What does it mean to have conversation full of grace? *Help children see that gracious speech involves gentleness, patience, love, kindness, and other ways of showing honor to someone.*

Application

The way we say our words can communicate honor to someone else. Communication involves both words and feelings. Sometimes the feelings match the words, but sometimes they don't. Imagine that you surprised me by setting the table. What if I came and said, "Thanks, _____, I'm very pleased." *(Say it in a sarcastic or derogatory tone of voice. Exaggerate your tone to make the negative feeling obvious.)* What was wrong there? Were my words okay? What about my feelings?

We can season our conversation in different ways. To show honor to someone we can attach good feelings to our words. Those good feelings will be passed on to others and help them to feel good too.

I have two more sets of cards. One set of cards has phrases for you to read, and the other set lists emotions. What I want you to do is take one card from each pile. Say the sentence using the feeling mentioned, and we will try to guess what the feeling is.

Have each person—children and parents—act out one of the cards. See if you can guess the feelings. Praise children for their performance. As children guess different feelings than intended, talk about how that was a good guess and how hard it is sometimes to perceive the feelings a person has when he or she speaks. For children who can't read, tell them the sentence and give an emotion word to demonstrate.

With older children, this exercise can be fun, especially when there is a contrast between the words and the feelings. Discuss ways to communicate a difficult message to someone using this idea of feelings.

How can nonverbal communication help us? How can it be dangerous? The way we use our words can add or take away honor in a situation. Let's pray together that God will give our family words this week that are seasoned just right. During the week simply ask the question, "Are you attaching honoring feelings to your words?"

family together time #7: discovering patterns in your relationships

Goal

To recognize that each person develops patterns of relating which trigger others to respond in predictable ways

Preparation

Prepare a poster that has the following information on it:

Trigger	Response
I want you to	*groan*
work or *clean*	*sigh*
no	*But, Dad…*
now	*Not yet!*

Come to the Family Together Time wearing a funny hat, dark glasses, or odd makeup. Take notes about how people respond when they see you're dressed funny. Note the nonverbal and verbal communication. The responses don't necessarily have anything to do with honor, but they communicate a message. Note big eyes, round mouth, raised eyebrows, hand movements, etc.

Review

In a minute I'm going to tell you why I look different, but first let's see if we remember what we learned last week. Last time we talked about messages we give, along with words, to communicate honor or dishonor. I took notes on the nonverbal messages and words people said when they saw my outfit. *List the things you heard and saw. Imitate them if possible. Family members will be surprised by your observations, and reviewing nonverbal communication should be a funny experience.*

Introduction

Every person develops habits of relating—these include body language, tone of voice, attitude, expressing anger or internalizing it, and so on. Let's try to put all the members of our family in order from most to least in the following areas.

Who has the most/least energy in the morning? at night?

Who needs the most/least sleep in our family?

Who talks the most/least in our family?

Who listens the best in our family?

Who does the most/least leading or giving instructions in our family?

This little quiz doesn't say anyone is good or bad. It just reveals differences. We all have different ways of relating to each other. In fact, others learn to expect us to relate the way we do. We usually take these things for granted.

What did you think when you saw me dressed funny like this? It was different, wasn't it. You didn't expect it.

We also have expectations in the way we relate to each other. What does Dad do when children are bickering? How does Mom handle it? How does one child get another to start fighting? These are areas where we see predictable patterns.

A Lesson from God's Word

We all have expectations about who people are and how they are going to act. Listen to what Jesus says in Mark 6:3-5:

> "Isn't this the carpenter? Isn't this Mary's son and the brother of James, Joseph, Judas and Simon? Aren't his sisters here with us?" And they took offense at him.
>
> Jesus said to them, "Only in his hometown, among his relatives and in his own house is a prophet without honor." He could not do any miracles there, except lay his hands on a few sick people and heal them.

What did the people think of Jesus? Why? What did Jesus say about families in general? Jesus was saying that honor isn't present in many families because people take each other for granted. We make assumptions about people and how they relate to us.

In all families we see predictable patterns in the way people relate. One area these patterns are clear is in conflict situations. Every person in a family has buttons that, when pushed, draw them into conflict. We call these pet peeves. Here are some examples. "I don't like it when Bobby drums his fingers on the table or kicks the chair over and over again. It's irritating." "When Patty pushes or pokes me, I get mad." "It's annoying when my little brother copies me all the time." All of these are triggers that draw us into conflict. Name some pet peeves that each family member has. *You may have to help children here because patterns and triggers are often hidden and subconscious, not easily seen.*

If we can find the buttons that others push on us we can learn to make changes in our responses. What are some things we can do instead of getting angry over pet peeves?

Application

Use the chart you made earlier to explain this activity. There are also a number of cues in the ways that parents and children relate to each other, especially when instructions are given. I just say a word, and a child has an immediate response. We're going to play a fun game to illustrate this.

I need four people to respond when I give cues. *Assign the responses to each person. If you don't have four people, then some may double up. Practicing this is fun even before you start. Encourage people to exaggerate their responses. Those who do a groan should also exhale heavily and be noisy. They might even roll their eyes at the same time. The person who sighs might shrug his or her shoulders at the same time. The person who says, "But, Dad!" should do so with a high, whiny voice. The person who says, "Not yet!" should do it with an exaggerated tone of voice.*

All right. I'll read the story, and you listen for cues. *As you read the story, pause and maybe even look to the child who is to give a response.*

> It's Saturday morning. Everyone knew that this would be a
> Saturday to **work** (sigh) in the yard. Dad was up early and got
> out the tools. He headed out front to start trimming some
> bushes. He had been outside for about an hour and decided it
> was time to have his two children, Craig, ten, and Marlene,
> twelve, join him.

"Craig, come on outside please."

Craig looked out the window. "What did you say, Dad?"

"*I want you to* help me in the yard." (groan)

Craig was having a difficult time getting himself going this morning. He liked to get involved in projects and often had a hard time switching when asked.

"Craig, we've got a lot of things to *clean* up out here." (sigh) "*I want you to* come give me a hand." (groan) "We can get a lot of *work* done today." (sigh)

Craig turned away from the window for a minute, then turned back and said, "Could I play on the computer a little longer?"

His dad looked up at him and said, "*No*." (But, Dad…) "We're going to do this *work*" (sigh) "*now*." (Not yet!)

When Craig came outside, Dad said, "*I want you to* get a broom…" (groan) "and *clean* the sidewalk." (sigh)

"Where's the broom?" Craig asked.

"Check in the shed to see if you can find it."

"Couldn't you get it for me, Dad? I'm tying my shoe."

"*No*," (But, Dad…) "*I want you to* go find it." (groan)

Just then Marlene came out. "What are you guys doing?" she asked.

"Today is the day we're going to get some things done around here. We could use your help. *I want you to* rake those leaves." (groan)

"Could I sweep instead, Dad?"

"*No*." (But, Dad…)

"Look, you guys. After we get all done, we're going to play

and have some fun together, but **now**" (Not yet!) "*I want you to*" (groan) "*work*." (sigh) "Let's not have any more complaining. We're going to **work**" (sigh) "for a while. *I want you to*" (groan) "do it **now**." (Not yet!)

That's a funny story. It's interesting to use triggers and responses that way. Do we have patterns like that in our family? It will be fun to watch our responses this week and see what we learn.

Watch for triggers and patterns in family relationships this week, and encourage honoring ways to respond to each other. When a child whines after a no answer or groans after an instruction, you might jokingly say, "Was that a trigger?" These small comments help children become aware of the ways they're relating.

End your time together in prayer.

family together time #6:
god rewards secretly

Goal

To recognize that God rewards us when we show honor even if no one else does

Preparation

Create a sign that reads, "Is this bathroom ready for the next person?"

Review

Last week we talked about patterns of communicating with triggers and responses. What new triggers did you notice this week? What is the definition of *honor?*

Introduction

What are some of the rewards honor brings to family life? *Allow family members to share. Some ideas include joy, peace in relationships, good feelings, satisfaction.*

Sometimes when you show honor, you receive a reward. What are some examples? *Asking in an honoring way is more likely to receive a yes answer. Other rewards include praise, recognition, or a good reputation.*

A Lesson from God's Word

Read the story about Mike and the lawn mower at the beginning of chapter four of this book. What two rewards did Mike receive when he showed honor by doing more than what was expected? Sometimes people don't see the things we do, and we don't get any credit for them. That's what we want to talk about today.

Read Matthew 6:1-4:

Be careful not to do your "acts of righteousness" before men, to be seen by them. If you do, you will have no reward from your Father in heaven.

So when you give to the needy, do not announce it with trumpets, as the hypocrites do in the synagogues and on the streets, to be honored by men. I tell you the truth, they have received their reward in full. But when you give to the needy, do not let your left hand know what your right hand is doing, so that your giving may be in secret. Then your Father, who sees what is done in secret, will reward you.

Jesus spoke these words to motivate people to please God even when they don't get any praise from people. Describe a time you did something that was honoring but didn't get noticed or didn't get a reward.

Application

One place we can show honor to others is in the bathroom. Honor means doing more than what's expected. *Move your meeting to the bathroom where you'll be able to see specific examples.* People are using the bathroom continually, and it tends to get messy. Sometimes people just walk out and say, "It's not my job." The result is a messy bathroom for the next person. Honor is important, even in the bathroom, so I've made this little sign to put here by the light switch. *Take the sign you made earlier, and tape it up.* What are some jobs that people could do before they leave the bathroom? *Close the cupboards, rinse out the sink, clear off the counter, put toilet paper on the roller, straighten the towels, and so on.* When you see this sign as you're leaving the bathroom, I want you to think about honor and doing more than what's expected. That means you may be cleaning up someone else's mess. Remember, others may not notice who's doing it, but God does, and he rewards those who show honor.

Final Review

What are some ways honor has affected our family in the last few weeks? *Share improvements parents have made as well.* What did we learn when we all got gifts but _____ got a gift of dirt first?

What are some of the different ways we can show honor? Gratefulness was learned in the story of the Pierson family. Valuing others as special, having a good attitude, and doing more than what's expected are other ways to show honor. What did we learn about honoring leaders?

Which Family Together Time did you enjoy the most, and why? *This could serve as a review of each of the topics and lessons you learned. End with prayer and the commitment to continue to grow in honor as a family.*